ב״ה

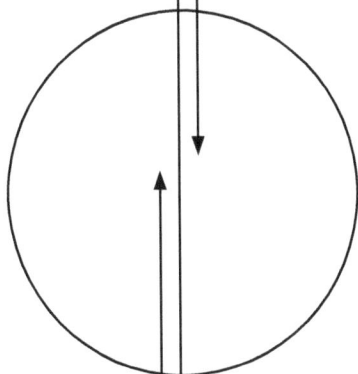

PROCESS + PRESENCE

Life in Balance

Rav Dovber Pinson

IYYUN
PUBLISHING

IYYUN PUBLISHING

Published by IYYUN Publishing
650 Sackett Street
Brooklyn, NY 11217

http:/www.iyyun.com

Iyyun Publishing books may be purchased for educational, business or sales promotional use. For information please contact: contact@IYYUN.com

Editor: Reb Matisyahu Brown

Editor: Reb Eden Pearlstein

Cover and book design: RP Design and Development

pb ISBN 978-1-7367026-8-0

Pinson, DovBer 1971-
PROCESS AND PRESENCE : Life in Balance

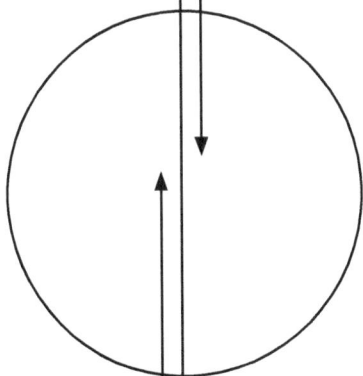

PROCESS
+
PRESENCE

Life in Balance

Rav Dovber Pinson

Exploring the essence of human fulfillment,
Process & Presence is the companion to a more
philosophical book by Rav Pinson, entitled
*The Garden of Paradox: The Essence of Non-Dual
Kabbalah in Three Conversations.*

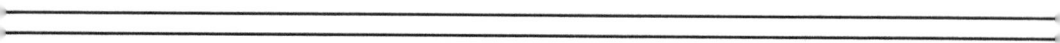

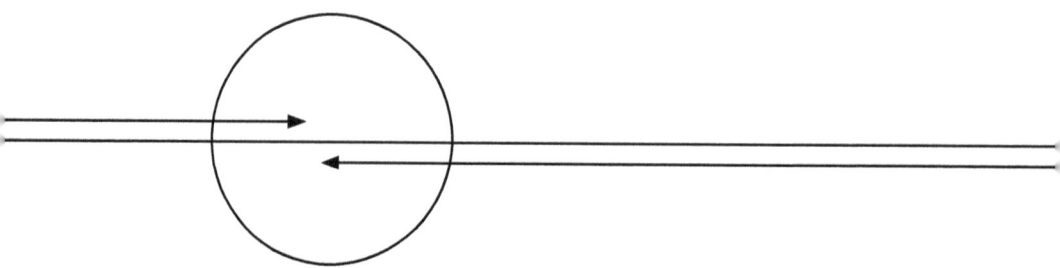

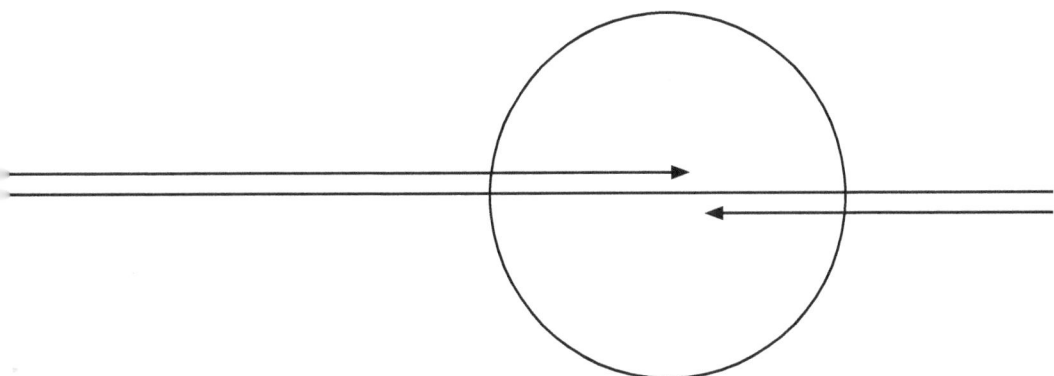

THIS BOOK IS DEDICATED
TO MY DEAR STUDENTS

Sam and Ashley Levinson שיחי׳

and their children

Izzy and Zeke שיחי׳

*With blessings for a life
of harmony and holiness.*

*May the Light of the Divine
shine upon you always.*

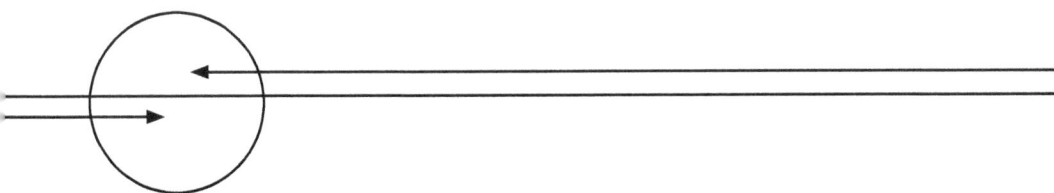

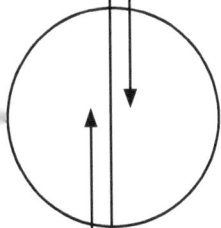

OPENING

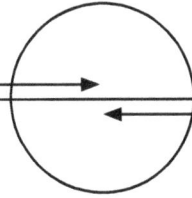

W E VIEW THE OBJECTIVE WORLD AROUND US THROUGH the subjective prisms of our own consciousness; we interpret and assimilate experience by means of our own state of mind. What we see on the outside is a reflection of what is happening on the inside. In general, there are two basic ways to experience the world: 'chaos' and 'order'. Either the world seems to be falling apart, or evolving toward a higher order — and this appearance depends on our own perception.

A gnawing sense of chaos, incoherence, purposelessness, or disjointedness clamors for the attention of most people. Despite this noise, a bedrock of interconnectivity, order, and meaning, also quietly supports human consciousness at all times. Even if we feel disoriented by the jutting stones along our life's path or chafed by seemingly unrelated shards of our story, we are all capable of catching at least a glimpse into the deeper coherence and peace within it all. Indeed, without an underlying sense of deep order, we could not function at all. To truly thrive in the midst of swirling chaos, we need to open ourselves to the dynamic of structural order.

On a deeper level, both order and chaos are true perspectives, and even helpful ones. In fact, to grow, we must experience both, with their complementary dynamics. Order provides comfort, security, and a steady sense of purpose and trajectory. It allows us to walk upright with a firm footing in this world. Yet, chaos urgently compels us to try to understand our life more deeply, it often stimulates us to submit to a higher calling and drives us to make new breakthroughs and discoveries. For example, the chaos created by the Black Death and the Great Plague was arguably the impetus behind the artistic and scientific breakthroughs of the Renaissance Era. By extension, the suffering of those times helped birth a more democratic, open society, and eventually freedom of religious practice.

We must pray for the end of all war, and the dawning of a time when "swords will be turned into plowshares and spears into pruning hooks." However, as terrible and horrific as war is, it also has the potential to thrust humanity to greater levels of conscience, harmony, and compassion.

In our own personal life, coherence without chaos can become too comfortable and lead to static stagnation. When everything is clear, orderly, and predictable, it can deaden our senses and cramp our creativity. Chaos without coherence, on the other hand, can lead to a fracturing of self, dissociation from others, and eventually, a frightening headlong dive into depression and nihilism.

Inwardly, the force of chaos may at times be felt as stress, but also unbridled, raw energy and ambition. Order, by contrast, may manifest as a sense of focus, organization, and contentment. When the contour of our life alternates between these two forces, we naturally strive for success and then, eventually, stop and settle down. In other words: *Stress brings us to rest*. Once we are regenerated, the urge arises to push ourselves again, out of this repose and into a higher layer of yearning and exertion, only to then settle later into a deeper state of satisfaction. Through such cycles of rest and exertion, we become more and more productive, reflective, creative, and deeply grounded.

ORDER EMERGES FROM CHAOS

In the Torah's description of the Creation story, order emerges from chaos. At first, the surface of the earth is covered with undifferentiated, chaotic waters, and then a process of 'separation' ensues. This process begins with the creation of light, which symbolizes the fundamental capacity to distinguish between phenomena. This draws out more and more 'orderly' qualities: day and night, water and dry land, and the celestial cycles which mark extended cycles of time. Finally, the culmination of this process — human life — is launched within a matrix of form meaning, self-awareness, and agency.

Later, when the Torah describes the infancy of Moshe, he is hidden in a river, and then drawn out of the water to eventually become the great liberator, guiding millions of people into higher coherence and meaning. A mass of water has no distinctions between its parts, no prevailing structure or form, yet Moshe, the man of wise law and order, emerges from the chaos of water. For each of us as well, the Torah illuminates a path out of constant chaos, and into a deeper life of peace, coherence, and meaning.

CHAOS IS 'PROCESS' AND ORDER IS 'PRESENCE'

Chaos is a churning sea of unbridled, raw ambition, like the boundless energy of a teenager or young adult, a person 'in process'. Order is the 'dry land', settled and cultivated, like the focused consciousness of a more mature, experienced, methodical person.

Just like the Creation narrative and the story of Moshe, our personal journey moves from chaos to order, from immaturity to maturity. As young children and adolescents, much of our lives are dominated by chaos; we are in the unsettled and unsettling process of becoming who we wish to be in this world.

Young or youthful people are more idealistic, bubbling over with a sense of restlessness and urgency, attuned to a powerful call to accomplish what has never been accomplished before. Many young people feel a stinging sense that society has failed until now, and that they must fix it all before the world self-destructs. The planet is on fire, and they are its only hope. As we grow older, we move into a more settled state of order, becoming more comfortable with who we truly are at the core of our being. This is a natural process of development that ideally leads us as we evolve from a state of chaos into one of order.

On a more psychological level, no matter our age, our own inner world can sometimes feel like it is falling apart at the seams. Our emotions and our relationships with others seem to be ruled by conflicts, passions, heartbreaks, high ambitions, and deep disappointments. From within this isolated and isolating state, we are driven to seek balance and a healthy connection with all our strength, to break free from our brokenness and pain.

At a certain point in this process, when we begin to mature, we may feel a deeper yearning for a sense of ease in our lives. Our body, mind, and soul cry out for peace, and we have a great urge to center ourselves, take a deep breath, and acknowledge, accept, and appreciate the fact that everything is already as it is meant to be. The harried pace of perpetual productivity exhausts itself and falls away, if only for short moments. The waters of chaos do eventually part, revealing the harmony of Creation, the kindness and care that nature gives to each tender blade of grass and flower petal, and the precise meal that the Creator prepares for every creature.

Witnessing all of this, we may be drawn into the stillness of contemplation, or a spontaneous perception of the majestic symmetry of the universe, and slip into a sense of radical wonderment. Merely holding a piece of bread can be a profound experience, as we contemplate the multitude of conditions and events that needed to sync up in order for this food to exist — from the balanced ecology and the human technology and economy that allowed the kernels of grain to grow and survive, nourished by the sun and soil, to be irrigated and skillfully harvested, dried and ground into flour. There had to be a precisely executed recipe and baking procedure, and proper storage and transportation, until finally the bread reached our hands. We realize, in that timeless moment, that we are witnessing a 'miracle' dressed in the garments of everyday reality; extraordinary coherence revealed within a seemingly chaotic world.

We might also contemplate the remarkable scientific knowledge of humanity, and see that it is all based on the sense that 'order' and universal laws do exist within our minds and within the world. We will eventually be able to see that there is a basic coherence between the universe and our own minds, enabling us to research, analyze, and come to conclusions about the world at large. Indeed, without a sense of inner order and an alignment between self and world, the very act of scientific exploration would not be possible.

We may also, with awe, spend time thinking about the myriad acts of human kindness. Someone is right now bending down to a helpless person and offering some food, even though they themselves do not have enough for the day. A child is courageously standing up for a classmate being bullied. A powerful nation is working to ensure the protection of another nation. A sense of shared humanity, of brotherhood and unity, seeps through and opens our consciousness to the spectacular goodness that underlies all of life.

Even when we do see the world falling apart and disintegrating, riddled by struggles between individuals, groups, and nations, the corruptions of power, and the tragedy of valuing profits over peace, there are nevertheless people coming together in open-hearted generosity. Strangers are sacrificing their comforts and resources to share, help, feed, house, and educate others, and to hold each other steady amid crises. Harmful boundaries are being broken down, compassion and love are being extended — Divine harmony and beauty are being revealed at this very moment if we would but notice.

Within our own private lives, too, we are often painfully pulled into different directions, from the competing demands of work, relationships, parenting, health, and self-development. One struggles to feel good enough and yet must also contend with their over-blown arrogance. One tries to be a good parent, yet their own inner child feels unconsoled; one strives to be a role model of virtue and patience to others, yet consistently falls into patterns of friction and frustration. And yet, at times, all the pieces come together, seemingly beyond reason or prediction. One day, we are walking down the street, and as if out of the blue, we are awash with the awareness that everything in our life actually makes sense — not 'logically', but rather viscerally and intuitively. Despite the very real stress, worry, and busy-ness of our lives, things feel perfect just as they are. A sense of well-being rises up, and with it, a fierce faith in life and in oneself.

One might even feel shattered and hopeless, yet, in the quiet depth of the night, there is a subtle sensation of calm in the background of consciousness. There is a deep feeling that despite everything, you are OK, you are whole, and everything in your life and in the world is unfolding exactly as it should be, and all is moving toward a greater good.

FISSION VS. FUSION

Nuclear *fission*, breaking apart atoms, has been a standard source of electric energy for many decades. Atomic and nuclear bombs, too, are created by fission. When two atoms slam into each other in a particular way, one of them is forced to break apart and split into two smaller atoms. For instance, when a smaller neutron collides with tremendous power with a uranium atom, the latter splits, unleashing tremendous energy, heat, and radiation. Other neutrons are released as well, and this causes a chain reaction in which these neutrons continue to collide with other uranium atoms. The power of splitting, breaking, and destroying is formidable.

On the other hand, physicists are currently developing a different technology: nuclear *fusion*. In this approach, two smaller atoms are made to collide in such a way that they join to form a heavier atom. For example, if two hydrogen atoms fuse, they can form one helium atom. Helium is the basis of the energy of the sun (*helios* in Greek). If such a procedure can be appropriately replicated, harnessed, and applied, it could produce unprecedented amounts of energy, and even be able to meet the power needs of the entire globe, all with much greater environmental and human safety than nuclear fission.

Such is the power of fusion or 'unification'. It is vastly more productive, clean, and coherent than fission or 'disunification'. At least subconsciously, we all seek to achieve fusion and mitigate fission, as we sense that unity is the very foundation of our existence and that of the entire cosmos. Clearly, it is advantageous to advance human and planetary thriving through unity and cooperation rather than through disunity and conflict.

PARTICLE VS. WAVE

In another area of scientific inquiry, every particle or quantum entity can either be described as a particle or as a wave.

At one time, in their quest to understand the physical universe, scientists focused on scrutinizing the minute differences between substances and dynamics. In the last hundred years or so, this has shifted toward discovering a unified theory of everything.

Ultimately, the wave perspective and the particle perspective are both true. Using them as metaphors for life, 'wave' means unity, and 'particles' imply separation. We need to access, embrace, celebrate, and connect with both perspectives; to practice both 'fission' and 'fusion', as it were.

The external world of particles, seeming chaos, disorder, and strife, can also be called the world of 'exile'. Our internal 'wave' world, of spirituality, order, unity, and fusion, can be called the world of 'redemption'.

EXILE & REDEMPTIVE STATES

From the perspective of exile, our reality lacks perfection, and we are driven to yearn, dream, and throw ourselves into the work of creating a better world and self. In this state, we are cognizant that we are 'not there yet', and complete wholeness is viewed as a future attainment. Our purpose is thus to aspire and constantly strive to reassemble the fractured 'particles' of reality into a coherent whole.

From the perspective of timeless unity and redemption, on the other hand, there is no separate 'future' to attain. No process of development is relevant, for all value is already present here, now, and in you. You *are* 'presence' and presence is infinitely everywhere and always. You come from and are born into eternal wholeness and perfection. Our higher consciousness, our soul, exists beyond the fluctuations of time and space. From that perspective, the 'future' redemption is always already present in the present. We can consciously assume this perspective if we calm the storm of our minds and tune into the underlying world of unity and wholeness. In fact, the very existence of all humanity, and by extension, the entire world, is rooted in unity. We are created within the Infinite Light of the Garden of Eden. As a reflection of this, every child, no matter the external circumstances of their lives, is deeply imbued with Paradise consciousness, floating weightlessly in the Eden-ic amniotic waters of their mother's womb. This peaceful state of fluidity, brilliance, and pure awareness never, in fact, leaves us.

Yet, the mere act of being born is traumatic; as we are born, we are jolted out of the Garden of Eden, so to speak. At first, the Garden just doesn't fit us anymore. We need more space to stretch and move. Then things begin shaking. Our mother's water breaks and drains away, we are thrust out of Eden and into the cold, the glare, the noise, the gravitational pull, and the rough surfaces of earthly life. We are separated from our home, our source of life, sustenance, and well-being. We cry and gasp for our first breath of oxygen, and our umbilical cord is abruptly cut, the first existential exile. Medical professionals might whisk us away from our mother and her warmth. One might be placed in a little plastic compartment to rest, or in a glass box for intensive care or observation. The familiar sounds and sensations of our previous environment are gone. For the first time, we are alone.

As we grow into a toddler, our path of development is to individuate; we gradually come to see ourselves as a separate individual, not an extension of our mother or parents. We go on mentally distinguishing and separating ourselves from others until we gradually enter a world of 'true exile'. We come to learn that some people are not trustworthy and that there are 'strangers' who could hurt us. We are sent to the unfamiliar surroundings of preschool and kindergarten, away from our family, left to negotiate relationships with other children, caregivers and teachers. After this ever-deepening experience of 'fission', if left unchecked or balanced, we can finally get a sense of being devastatingly lost in a gaping abyss, dissociated from the here and now, and, sadly, even from our own self.

EMPTINESS & EXILE AS POWERFUL FUEL

Children are, in general, highly adaptive and resilient; however, through the naturally occurring path of 'fission' and exile, an insatiable desire for 'fusion' kicks in. One begins to feel that if they could only obtain a certain toy or experience, they would feel less empty. Such desires eventually develop into the fierce idealism or darkness of youth. Eventually, these energies morph into the constant struggles of adult life to climb higher on social, economic, or professional ladders. Sometimes, one may also begin to focus on growing spiritually or emotionally. Finally, one yearns to retire and rest and have all one's needs taken care of by others. During this entire trajectory, we strain mightily to lift from upon us the heavy fallout of 'fission', constantly attempting to return, in any way we can, from exile to our original Edenic comfort and glow.

Yet, even deep within this life of effort — even right now — you may look within and locate a sense that you are already 'home'. However you define it, deep down, at the very base of our experience, you may recognize that you are already fulfilled, whole, perfect, and complete, just as you are. All is, in fact, well. Your spiritual studies and contemplations are but unveilings of this truth that is already the case: there is no need to do anything to return to Eden. It is who you already are and always have been.

WE ARE BOTH:
PROCESS / EXILE &
PRESENCE / REDEMPTION

Exile and redemption are real and valid perspectives. Just as light is simultaneously wave and particle, we are both whole and fractured, in a state of redemption and of exile. The question is, how can we live with both perceptions?

In a state of 'process', we have not yet arrived, the world is still broken, and one still does not yet have enough love, money, or power. We strenuously strive to improve our lives and make the world a better, happier, more just, and Divine place.

In a state of 'presence', we have already arrived; there is nowhere to go, no reason to fight. Everything is perfect as it is....

The answer is that we must remain sensitive to suffering, imperfection, and 'exile', yet engage with it from within a greater understanding of well-being, perfection, and 'redemption'. For example, inwardly, we may be living in peace and serenity, gratitude and blessing, relief and resolution; however, this should not eclipse the fact that there are people outside who are still cold, frightened, alone, living in literal or mental scarcity and hunger. The truth is, we cannot ignore the pain of the exterior world and remain fully absorbed in a cocoon of inner peace; at some point, we will be pulled out of ourselves and into the world.

Throughout this text, we will explore the path of 'process', and the pathless path of 'presence', through various lenses. We will hold these dialectical states of consciousness simultaneously:

Duality *and* unity,

Becoming *and* being,

Brokenness *and* wholeness,

Action *and* rest,

Motion *and* stillness,

Striving *and* satisfaction,

Lack *and* fullness,

Wanting *and* having,

Vulnerability *and* strength,

Compassion *and* contentment.

01

PROCESS & PRESENCE WITHIN THE SELF:
LAYERS OF CONSCIOUSNESS

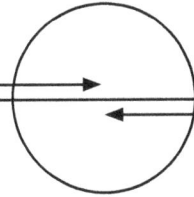

SELF-KNOWLEDGE IS KEY TO ANY TYPE OF EMOTIONAL, mental, or spiritual growth. We need to know who we are in order to know who we want to become. In fact, what distinguishes us as human beings from all other animals on the planet is our ability to self-reflect, obtain self-knowledge, and as a result, to have a capacity for free choice.

Clearly, if we don't yet know ourselves we can't move forward or accomplish meaningful goals because we cannot yet make choices based on our unique constellation of abilities and character traits, gifts, and challenges. We need to clarify who and what we are and build from there. A child may think he wants to be a firefighter when he grows up, but this idea may have little relation to his actual skills, strengths, and sensibilities. It may not at all correspond to who he is. Only as he matures and learns about himself and is able to more sensitively sense his calling, do his choices and self-direction become relevant.

To reach a more profound level of self-knowledge, we must engage in methodical investigation and reflection, deconstructing our assumed identities and false narratives. When untruths are exposed, they can be released, and we can begin to clarify what is real and true.

EXAMINING OUR IDENTIFICATION WITH OUR BODY

To discover more clearly who we are, let us start by examining the nature of what virtually all of us identify as: our body. For many, their physicality is the primary component of their sense of value. The more beautiful or capable their bodies appear to be, the more confident they are. Sadly, the opposite is also the case: the less beautiful someone thinks they are, the less confident they feel. Not only our self-image but our very sense of self is often tied to the ever-fluctuating state of the body.

Shorter people may develop what some call a 'Napoleon complex', a domineering attitude developed as a kind of overcompensation for being physically slight. Taller people may subliminally think they are powerful just because they can see over others' heads. Heavier people may feel a need to bolster their self-esteem by excelling intellectually or cultivating an outstanding sense of humor. Thinner or fitter people may feel more confident and entitled. But behind all these empty posturings, anxieties, and assumptions, what is the body really?

In its widest definition, you can understand your body as a collection of cells working in harmony to form a larger unit, which has the label "mine" on it. "My body." Put more bluntly, it is a wiggly 150-pound (on average) bag of protoplasm that usually hovers between 98 and 99 degrees Fahrenheit. We can see and feel it, and seemingly maneuver it as we desire, at least some of the time.

But can this bag of protoplasm be the real you? If you think so, contemplate the following scenarios. If you donate blood, a living tissue that is an essential part of your body, do you experience 'yourself' flowing within the veins of the person who received the transfusion? Say a person loses a hand or foot. Does that person in any way become less 'them' than they were prior to the injury? Certainly not. So what, where, and who is the real you? If you are not defined by any one of your parts — your blood, arms, legs, toes, or fingers — then why assume that you are the sum total of these individual parts?

Perhaps you sense that you are inside your head, that you are your brain; for if your brain was removed from your body, you feel you would no longer be you. However, if just certain parts of your brain were removed, perhaps you would lose many cognitive and motor functions, but you would remain 'you'. In deep, dreamless sleep, as well, you don't have cognitive and motor functions. However, when you wake up, you still have the same name, childhood memories, and shopping list. You weren't 'deleted' and then replaced by a different you. Somehow you remained you even while your brain was neither thinking nor telling your body to sit, stand, or walk.

If you still feel that you are located somewhere within your brain, where exactly in the brain are you? In the rear or the front of the brain? Assuming you feel like you are located in the front of your brain, how many inches deep do you extend from the front surface, and how many inches wide are you? Maybe about 2.5 inches? Do you really walk around thinking of yourself as a 2.5-inch wide ball behind a pair of eyes? When someone asks you how tall you are, do you say you've never actually measured, but probably about 2.5 inches? Obviously, your brain is not you, nor is any part of it. It's just an organ that serves 'you' with some vital functions.

For argument's sake, let's return to the premise that you are the sum total of all the parts of your body. Now contemplate the fact that the materials of your body are constantly being replaced and regenerated. 98 percent of the atoms in your body were not there one year ago. Your skin is renewed every month; your stomach lining, every four days; and the surface cells that come into contact with food, every five minutes. Zooming into the sub-nuclear level, the elements that make up your atoms, the quarks and gluons, are perpetually being annihilated and recreated. So, in fact, you never have the same body as even a moment ago, yet you claim to be the same self as moments, and even years and decades, ago: "*I* was born in 1990..." as one might say.

It is a bit peculiar to establish a persistent sense of identity as something that does not persist over time.

Even to your own eye, your body looks and feels a little different from month to month and year to year. How can *you* be your body if your body is always different? One thing is clear: you are always exactly you. Your you-ness doesn't change or get wrinkles. You never become someone else and then need to report your previous self to the authorities as a missing person. If your body is currently aging to some extent, the body you had when you were a young child is no longer present, but you are still present. *You* are essentially what is *always* present in your direct experience.

Identifying yourself with the body alone should now be completely ruled out. Feel the inner effects of having deconstructed or released the belief that you are, in essence, a body. Perhaps there is a subtle sensation of stillness, lightness, or presence at this moment; perhaps there is a subtle sense of tumult in having dethroned an impostor, a fake 'you'. If you feel upset or dissociated, take a break or talk to a friend. Know that the goal of this process is an all-inclusive wholeness embracing your physical aspect, and you are not being asked to sever yourself from anyone or anything of value. Deconstructing previous perspectival limitations should only serve to enhance your sense of well-being, vitality, and appreciation for the miracle of embodiment. The goal is to see through 'process' enough to glimpse 'presence'.

EXAMINING IDENTIFICATION WITH THOUGHTS & EMOTIONS

After verifying that our true identity is not our body, the next candidate is our thoughts and feelings. Thoughts form our narratives and limiting self-definitions, and create or stimulate our emotions.

In direct experience, where do your thoughts come from? Can you find them waiting in the wings, ready to appear on the stage of the mind? Does any one thought or moment of feeling define or encapsulate the totality of you? Of course not.

Now that we have deconstructed the basic misidentifications with body and mind, we can rise above them, and gain a more inclusive view of who we are as a person, a 'process'. We can take a fresh look and see previously obscured details of our personality and experience that were eclipsed by our false sense of self. We can also begin to see what we are as 'presence', our prevailing deeper nature beyond the perpetual 'process' of our constantly evolving personality.

KNOWING OUR 'PROCESS SELF'

We see ourselves and the world around us, for better or worse, based on the mindset we entertain. There is a prism through which we process experiences; we see them not the way they are, but the way *we* are, the way our thoughts, emotions, beliefs, and needs overlay and interpret reality.

This prism is constantly in flux and evolution. When a person is young, their mindset, and the thoughts they have, are very different than when they are older. This is the layer of self that is constantly growing in awareness and information, understanding, and responsiveness. From this perspective, we are engaged in an ongoing process of physical, mental, emotional, and spiritual development, thus we could call this part of self our 'process-self' or our 'autobiographical self'.

Self-discovery on this level requires getting to know the 'what' of our changing experience. What are your central desires, yearnings, ambitions, and goals? What makes you 'you', with all your uniqueness? What makes you tick, what makes you alive, alert, engaged, and inspired? And by contrast, what deadens or alienates you? What shuts you down, challenges, or frightens you? The answers to these questions, and more, make up the 'what' of who you are. Of course, we also need to see into the deeper regions of our process-self, the 'how' and the 'why' of our personality. We need to understand how our early memories and experiences formed patterns in our life. The quality of our narrative changes dramatically when we see how our choices were inspired, and why we cultivated certain skills and needs and relationships, and not others.

To become more aware of the process-self, it helps to keep a journal. Take ten minutes a day on weekdays to briefly note on paper what you want, how you feel, and any predominant thoughts, questions, or emotional triggers that you are experiencing today.

What are the thought patterns and emotions that arose today? What thoughts precipitated your emotions, and what actions flowed from these experiences? When did such patterns of action, thought, and experience first appear in your life? What were they in response to? Note the tone and content of your relationships. How do these relate to your relationships earlier in life?

While this level of knowing yourself is vital, self-knowledge goes beyond it as well. All the above allows us to be aware of our narratives, our thoughts and feelings, but who is having these thoughts? Who is the thinker, the feeler, the experiencer? Who or what witnesses all of these fleeting phenomena?

We need to discover the unchanging essence that precedes and witnesses all of our changing experiences and prisms.

OUR 'PRESENCE', OUR WITNESS SELF

We have seen that all our experiences, as well as our body and our brain, are in constant states of flux, always changing. But is there something about us or within us that never changes?

To attune to the unchanging frequency within the self, pause for a few moments and reverse your attention, turning away from the 'content' of experience — away from 'things', experiences, and narratives — toward the background awareness, that 'non-thing' which is seeing itself.

Confirm for yourself: this formless clarity, which registers everything that appears, never changes. Change happens 'within' it, yet it does not change. Even your body and mind appear within this clear, unchanging awareness. It is like the formless space in which a breeze blows. The air moves, but the space itself does not move.

In Hebrew, this witnessing 'I' is called *Da'as* / awareness, 'knowingness'. The letters in the word *Da'* / 'be aware' or 'know', can be rearranged to spell *Eid* / witness, referring to this empty witnessing, that which 'knows' experiences.

Pure awareness is not affected by anything that appears within it, just as the breeze does not in any way affect the open space in which it blows. Pure Da'as is not an object; it is empty of objective qualities. Thus, the witnessing self is empty of the 'objects' of thoughts, words and stories, feelings, images, sounds, impressions and experiences, identities, needs, forms, structures, filters, prisms, levels, and qualities.

Everything that appears to us comes and goes, rises to consciousness, and then disappears, while the 'I' of ever-pure awareness never comes nor goes. It is ever-present; it is presence. No suffering or misdeed can ever maim or modify the presence that you are. Detached and empty of all forms, you are the presence that is watching the myriad forms of your process-self as they change and unfold.

YOU & NOT-YOU

It is important to recognize that whatever is *known* cannot be you, the *knower*. By the very fact that we are aware of our body and bodily sensations, our thoughts and perceptions, it is obvious that we are not our bodies, nor our sensations, thoughts, or perceptions. Whatever can be observed is, by definition, not the observer. Whatever you are conscious of cannot be you. If you know your thoughts, then you cannot *be* your thoughts. If you know your passions, emotions, desires, and mistakes, you cannot be them either. You are pure awareness itself.

Da'as is the *experiencer*, as opposed to the experience,

The *feeler*, as opposed to the feeling,

The *observer* of thoughts, as opposed to the thoughts....

Anyone who has ever dabbled in any type of meditative technique, or for that matter in the philosophy and mechanics of the mind, knows that while thought appears to have 'a mind of its own', there are levels of being that are 'behind' the mind. When a person tells himself to think a particular thought, it is one level of the mind telling the more surface level what to think. And yet, having an awareness of both the depth and the surface of the mind tells us that there is still a deeper level of consciousness that experiences the mind.

Take a moment and look at the wall in front of you. Now, become aware of the level of mind that is aware of that looking. Then, 'step back' again and become aware of the fact that you are aware of the looking. You are aware of being aware.

One can keep stepping back again and again, ad infinitum, becoming aware of each previous state of awareness, like the infinite regression of a mirror reflecting another mirror. This is because the mind tends to reify and construct an 'image' of awareness, as if it is another 'thing', something that can be pictured. This is a subtle form of mental 'idolatry', so to speak, constructing a *Yesh* / existence, an image, out of imageless *Ayin* / no-thing-ness. However, with practice, one can simply cease constructing such 'things', or assuming that the present awareness is another 'thing', another layer of awareness, another Yesh. In this way, you can step back *only once* and realize that there is but one awareness, without levels or layers.

Awareness can never be grasped because it is that which 'grasps'. It can never truly be understood because it is that which understands. The 'seer' cannot be seen as an image; otherwise, it is not the seer of images. The knower cannot be known as an object, for it is the pure subject, knowing itself. And yet, mysteriously, we are aware that we are aware.

YESH-SELF & AYIN-SELF:
NARRATIVE AND DETACHMENT

Our autobiographical self, composed of finite experience, is called *Yesh* / finite existence. This is the self as 'process', ever unfolding and evolving. The witness-self is called *Ayin* / no-thing-ness or formless openness. As the Ayin-self, you are not a 'thing'; you are empty of descriptions, transcendent of the finite, definable stuff of life. This is the self as 'presence'.

All emotions, including love, are defined and finite in nature. When we can step back and bear witness, we can become aware of an emotion such as anger from a place of purity and detachment. When we are the *observer* of anger, we are not shackled to or by it. We are free from the drama of life. There is no personal 'meaning' or interpretation of phenomena in the impersonal no-self of Ayin; we don't take anything personally. In this way, anger is not really anger; it is just a passing and impersonal sensation, a finite thought form, that is watched as it rises and falls away within an endless ocean of peace.

As the observer, aware of our experiences as they pass through the present moment, we can come to know the nature of a given experience, what it is composed of, and what its causes and dynamics are.

For example, if we mindfully observe our emotions, we can examine them very deeply: what is an emotion? If we look deeply within the 'feeling' of a present emotion, we will see it is nothing more than physiological sensations, the raw data of uninterpreted sensory perception. This may be termed the *Chomer* / 'raw matter' of the emotion. On the outermost surface of an emotion is the "narrative," the story that the brain claims to be the cause of the sensations. When we examine this, we will see it is basically just words, mental images, and interpretations based on our beliefs. This outer expression can be called the *Tzurah* / form of the emotion.

In this process of mindful analysis, we can 'separate' the sensation from the narrative, the raw 'matter' from the 'form' of the emotion. If one is experiencing fear, they can separate the story of '*why* I am afraid' from the physical sensations in the body, and understand that both ingredients are, in themselves, not the 'fear'. Once they can deconstruct the fear into a combination of inert ingredients, it is much less triggering, and it may even dissolve. In either case, now the fear might not lead to an unwanted reaction in speech or deed. This practice can leave one with a greater sense of equanimity, and a profound realization that 'I am not my emotions.'

Whenever we are burning with emotions, frustrations, or infatuations, we can immerse in the vantage point of our Ayin-self, the detached observer, and view our emotions as neutral, raw data. Viewing ourselves in this way can even be mildly amusing, like watching a film or a spectator sport, observing without investment or excitement.

To the extent that the world of emotions, thoughts, and experiences is 'finite' and has 'form', the observing self is 'infinite' and prior to form. It feels very freeing to be in alignment with this 'infinity' within. We can untangle ourselves from emergent dramas by turning inwards to simply witness and dispassionately observe them. Additionally, we can loosen the hold that any past hurt or drama has upon us, by conjuring up the images, words, and sensations again, but this time, just observing them from the vantage of transcendent awareness.

Here is a practical way to use this awareness of process and presence, Yesh and Ayin. Any time you feel yourself being drawn into conflict, anger, jealousy, low self-esteem or unhealthy craving, stop. Stop reacting, stop spinning, stop perpetuating—pull your consciousness back to pure, impersonal awareness, and just rest there, passively observing all sense data from the no-place of *Ayin* / ungraspable emptiness of form and content.

As Ayin, we are not different from anyone else; we are just the borderless space of being. This is also called *Chayah* / transcendent aliveness. It is an endlessly powerful, undifferentiated potential, unchanging living presence empty of all thoughts, desires, attachments, wants, and vulnerabilities; free of impurities, mistakes, personal traits, and death. While this is a deeply life-giving reservoir to visit when needed, it is not a place to reside, as it is also free of all ambition, discipline, intellect, empathy, and even virtue.

OUR ESSENTIAL SELF

Amazingly, there is a level of self that is even deeper than the transcendence and infinity of 'presence'. This can be termed 'essence'. Our essential self is what comprises both the Yesh-self and the Ayin-self; it unifies the process-self and the presence-self in a paradoxical whole that is greater than the sum of its parts. To be accurate, essence is not as much a 'level' of self as it is the totality and actuality of what we are, including and transcending all individual levels. It is referred to as *Yechidah* / 'the singular'.

Yechidah is the deepest 'I', independent of environmental influences and physical identities, although it can include those experiences as well. In this way, it is the 'oneness' of content and context. It is a paradoxical unity of our psychophysical form and our formless awareness, our fullness and emptiness, our 'no-thingness' and 'somethingness', our 'process' and 'presence'. The essence of our being, our Yechidah, is one with the Essence of All, but it is also the unchanging, ageless sense of 'I' that we have been our whole lives. When we were young, we said, 'I am young,' and when we are old, we will say, 'I am old.' The 'I' referenced is the same 'I', regardless of the state of the body or the period of the body's lifespan. This timeless I is the eternal soul that exists before birth, during life, and after death.

Yechidah is the singular 'I' of all existence, the essential being within all life. Yet, it is not limited to the timeless, infinite, or transcendent aspect of our 'presence self'; it is simultaneously the 'process-self' of personal thoughts, feelings, and impressions. Yechidah embraces the fluctuations and limitations of our 'process' and personality. On the other hand, Yechidah should not be confused with ego or egoic ambitions and desires. It can experience ego but is paradoxically free from ego.

Our essential self manifests as our unique individual 'personality' and experience of life. A person who fully realizes that they are Yechidah still has ambitions similar to other individuals, only they are rooted in a transcendent detachment from the outcome. Such a person can have a tremendous drive to succeed, but not out of existential anxiety, lack, or desire for honor. They can even strive for 'self-improvement', yet without any restlessness or sense of deficiency. To be human is to be finite — a finite expression of the Infinite Creator.

The Infinite One desires to be expressed in finitude, multiplicity, differentiation, and personal uniqueness. Thus, each one of us has a 'unique' soul, as it were. The I of the Creator, expressed within our process-self, is who we essentially are: Yechidah.

TRANSPARENCY OF EGO

While ego is an infamous part of the lowest regions of the process-self, it is not in itself negative. It is, in fact, integral to human existence as it generates vital powers and drives necessary for survival and self-preservation. Every living being has an 'ego'; even a flower and a blade of grass. A blade of grass seeks out and 'competes' for water and sunlight so it will survive. It also seeks ways to perpetuate its species. Survival and perpetuation are two basic expressions of the 'ego' of every living organism.

Our body and mind are heavily programmed with natural egoic functions and inclinations. For example, a craving for chocolate might sometimes be a symptom of a nutritional need for magnesium or another natural compound. Besides the fact that chocolate is not the only source of dietary magnesium and that it contains the stimulant theobromine and often some amount of habit-forming sugar, the nutritional aspect of the craving can be an *adaptive* reaction of the body.

It could be argued that most egoic cravings are not fundamentally negative in nature; they are likely to be attempts of the system to fill a real need, whether that be certain nutrients or neurochemicals, friendship, or rest.

What's more, even if someone did consider the basic structure of ego negative and tried to eliminate it, they would not be able to; the self cannot eliminate itself. A wise Chasidic master once said that if you think you can break your 'negative' ego and try to do so, you will just wind up with two negatives instead of one: A) The ego will remain, for it doesn't just disappear, and B) arrogance arises from the very thought that 'you' could, or did, get rid of your ego.

The desire to get married, go out and make a living, make something of your life, or fulfill the basic needs of your body and of your family is positive. The trouble arises when these drives are not properly balanced with an expansive sense of transcendence. When people are self-centered in their relationships, they become at least subtly abusive, and their business dealings become exploitative. What began as an adaptive drive for fulfillment can end up as an excuse for terribly destructive behavior. One can maladapt their natural inclinations, passions, and needs until they become inclinations for evil.

The following is an extreme example of the descent from 'ego' to 'evil'. Many psychiatrists and criminologists studying some of the shadier characters of society conclude that there is a common disposition found in most of them: lack of an ability to be empathetic. They are unable to understand in their mind or feel in their heart the pain of another human being, and they cannot see themselves in others. There are also some criminals who are in a sense empathetic, in that they understand the pain they cause; however, they actually revel in causing that pain. These people lack compassion and the basic human desire to *not* cause suffering.

Both lack of empathy and lack of compassion originate from excessive self-centeredness and narcissism. Individuals who frequently act out of anger or hatred begin to feel god-like. They may even believe they have the power and the right to decide whose life is dispensable and whose life is significant. Sadly, it is not necessary to illustrate this with an example, since such horrifying stories appear frequently in the news media. Such people are so entangled and intoxicated with themselves and their uncontrolled thinking that they cannot see past themselves. Every relationship they have is not with a 'person', but with an object to be used or abused for their own ends.

While the preoccupation with oneself generally manifests as narcissism or hubris, it can also show up as a lack of self-worth. It can be argued that narcissistic 'arrogance' is, in fact, compensation for self-loathing. One's demands to be noticed are nothing but the psychological self-defenses of a deeper sense of existential lack. In any event, whether one shows exaggerated self-esteem or a complete lack of self-esteem, one is highly preoccupied with his egoic self.

Still, despite the conflicts engendered by egoism, the ego is not purely negative at its root; it is imperative to possess the drives and capacities for self-defense, competition, and the attainment of wholesome desires. Our task, then, is not to destroy the ego. Our task is to make the ego a transparent vessel that reveals our essence. It is to unify our process-self with our presence-self, integrating the ambitions and desires of Yesh with the contentment and serenity of Ayin. It is to reveal the field of being, our essence-self, that contains and holds formlessness and form in perfect harmony.

'SMALL I' AND 'BIG I'

Ego can also be called 'the small i', while our essential self, our soul, can be called 'the big I'. The root purpose of my 'small i' ambitions and desires is to motivate me to express myself in my own unique way, to contribute to the world, and to propel me to follow my deepest callings from the place of my soul. When the small i is thus in service of the big I, my desires, longings, and ambitions are not at the expense of other people. Rather, they are rooted in my essential abundance and wholeness, and they naturally increase abundance and wholeness for both myself and others.

A transparent ego, one fully in service of the big I, is not locked into a 'me-or-you' or 'us-or-them' worldview. It functions in a mode of 'me *and* you' and 'us *and* them'. There is an underlying faith that there is enough abundance to go around and no urgent need to hoard resources and push others away. There is a tangible sense that each of us is the Infinite One revealing Itself in the world through the frame of our unique lives and journeys. Living from the depths of who we ultimately are allows us to recognize the ultimate depth in others. We see their Divine potential, their inner 'infinity', and also appreciate their particular finite expression of the Infinite One.

The path towards self-actualization and fulfillment is ultimately about learning to live in accordance with the 'infinite' spark of the Divine that is made distinctly present within our own finite, individual life. The One Self pulsates within each of us in all our diversity and distinctiveness.

Just as no two people are identical physically, so too spiritually. Everyone is exceptional in his or her own way. Every soul has a spiritual vocation and mission that can only be fulfilled by that person alone.

The individual way that each person experiences the world is rooted in the uniqueness of their soul. Also, through the uniqueness of our soul, we uniquely influence the world. With every action, we imprint the 'seal' of our soul upon people, places, objects, and events. Every relationship we engage in is colored by who we are.

As Yechidah, we are standing on 'both sides of the door' simultaneously; we are not defined by our finite self nor our infinite 'no-self' — we are beyond this division, we are neither and both. Yechidah is an *inclusive* transcendence. In relationships, there is a transcendence of the small 'i' and a clear sense of a more expansive 'we'; yet I am uniquely I, and you are uniquely you. Spiritually, our inclusively transcendent 'uniqueness' is in perfect harmony with the Inclusively Transcendent Unique One, the Unity of All Reality. Thus, living out your most authentic uniqueness is fulfilling the very point of your reason for existing. Revealing our personal uniqueness in full detail reveals the Unique One in the myriad details of all existence.

THE SENSATION OF HIGHEST CONSCIOUSNESS AWARENESS

In this wonderful, almost paradoxical awareness and living, from the deepest part of self and soul, the place that unites process and presence, arises both ardent action and restful stillness.

The visceral sensation of living our deepest selves — beyond ego, and even beyond witnessing consciousness — is a taste of the perfection of life. You can be walking down the street, and all of a sudden, you get a sense that everything in your life is OK, coherent, and perfectly in order.

Some days you may be immersed in your narrative self and feel troubled by the chaos or seeming randomness of life. So many important needs are vying for your attention: being a good friend, a good parent, a good son or daughter, a good employee or boss or manager; doing well in business, wanting to grow and engage in study, prayer, meditation, and inner work. There are so many moving parts, it is impossible to juggle them all. You may feel your actions are disjointed, and your consciousness is misaligned. And then, one morning, you are taking out the garbage, and something hits you: 'Wow, life is actually in harmony! All the pieces of the puzzle fit together!' This is a flash of spiritual awakening; it is a glimpse of your inner perfection, the paradoxical unity of your process and presence, the deepest level of your soul shining through.

THREE LEVELS OF LIVING

In practical terms gleaned from the above discussion, there are three basic levels or ways of living: 1) Attachment to experience, 2) detachment from experience, and 3) 'radical re-engagement', meaning healthy re-attachment to experience.

1. Level One is the ego of our 'process-self'. On this level, we are invested deeply in our narrative, ambitions, and desires. We strive with life, and due to that we live with strife. When things don't go our way, we become anxious, our mind filled with thoughts such as, 'Am I doing the right thing? Am I a failure?' Whatever you are doing, and whatever level of expertise you reach, you may still find yourself second-guessing yourself. Whether you are working on creating, investing, producing, advising, or organizing, you can be consumed with doubts: 'Will I be successful? What do my clients really think of me? Are people interested in what I have to offer? Am I really capable of helping others? I still need help, myself!'

   Here you are attached to the drama of events and desperately trying to predict outcomes. Your list of unfulfilled needs seems endless. Sometimes you engage in great efforts to get what you want, and sometimes you collapse and give up on ever finding what you seek.

Every emotion you feel sweeps you away. When you are angry, no one can even speak to you, and you cannot calm yourself down. When you are elated or infatuated with some possibility, you are obsessed, and you clutch onto that sense of positivity or achievement.

Your highs are very high, and your lows are very low. Your attachment to 'process' conceals the underlying reality of 'presence'.

2. Level Two is your egoless 'presence self'. On this level, you retreat into a pure witnessing of your life, and hence you allow your life to pass over you as you sit silently observing, detached and unmoved by it all. You may take notice of your thoughts, emotions, and sensations, but you don't identify with them, and they fall away. If you feel yourself getting caught up in an emotion or a thought, you merely step back and observe it as if from afar.

As you transcend your process-self, you may get the feeling that you are 'enlightened'. Your emotions may become more even or perhaps flat, your worldly ambitions dissolve, and you perceive a lightness, an emptiness, and temporariness in all experience.

Individuals and communities that focus on living full-time in this perception may indeed have a feeling of profound inner peace, spiritual pleasure, and presence of mind. However, they may also dissociate from their needs and the needs of others. Some people have identified so exclusively with pure awareness that they have dropped out of society and found themselves sitting on a park bench for months, absorbed in blissful nothingness. Some extreme mystics have even become so absorbed in 'no-self' that they did not eat or move for long periods of time, and eventually needed to be rescued and fed by others. With no attachments of any kind, they were no longer functioning as physical beings.

While periodic self-transcendence is refreshing and indeed healthy, such as in deep sleep or prayer, permanently dwelling in transcendence can prevent one from personal growth or serving the world beyond the self. All medical, scientific, technical, and industrial breakthroughs, as well as all creativity and effective problem-solving, have manifested through people dipping even briefly into some form of transcendence and then bringing their refreshed consciousness back into the world. Such innovators purposefully return from their moment of transcendence back into their investment in human life, and to a sense of 'attachment' and ambition. Both transcendence and a healthy competitive drive are often instrumental in pushing a new abstract insight into usable form.

3. Level Three is living from both these levels of being, 'process' and 'presence', simultaneously. Yesh and Ayin are simultaneously expressed, revealing a harmony between the two, and manifesting a third stage of integration that is greater than the sum of the two. We have termed this 'essence', Yechidah, 'what you really are'. It can also be called 'radical

re-attachment', meaning attachment to experience from a place of non-attachment, a posture that integrates process and presence.

When you are consciously acting from your essence, you can actually encompass pain and transcend pain at the same time. To truly love your spouse or friend, for example, you open yourself up to their pain or stress and listen to their requests; you do not just sit there with eyes closed, zoned out, and unresponsive. This doesn't mean that you need to become anxious and abandon your inner wholeness or pure witness state whenever your loved one is in need of attention. You can be both fully empathetic and fully rooted in the well-being of pure consciousness.

If your child is having a terrible nightmare in the middle of the night, you do not stay reveling in the peaceful repose of sleep; you naturally leap up from bed and rush to comfort them. These movements may appear identical to attachment, restlessness, or anxiety, however, it is not necessarily so. A mature sense of responsibility may be rooted in peace and presence even when there is some sense of necessary urgency or alacrity.

If one is sustaining a family, he or she may go through the motions of striving for wealth in order to nourish and empower them with greater opportunities. Yet, this striving can be free from any egoic attachment to wealth or success: "Who is truly wealthy? One who is happy with what they already have." Indeed, wealth is a state of mind, in which a person lives with a sense of abundance and bounty.

In the coming chapters, we will explore the remarkable phenomenon of ambition without anxiety, striving from within stillness, speaking from within silence, and dancing beyond-and-within the dramas of life.

02

PROCESS & PRESENCE WITHIN TIME:

LINEAR TIME AND THE ETERNAL PRESENT

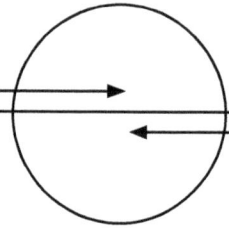

J UST AS OUR CONSCIOUSNESS HAS DIMENSIONS OF 'process' and 'presence', plus a third integral level, 'essence', which unites the two — so does our experience of time.

There are different ways of viewing time and the present moment. In the conventional, linear view, we are either unavoidably affected by a defined past or inevitably pulled toward an undefined future. Both of these paradigms are enfolded within the 'process' or Yesh aspect of time; there is a past moving into the present, and also a present moving into the future. This is time as a line.

YESH TIME & BEING CONTROLLED BY A DEFINED PAST

'Yesh-time' is the linear process of the past imprinting the present and the future. From this perspective, the present is the totality of the past accumulated in this current moment. The content of this moment is thus inevitable, as it is the 'birth' that issues from the 'impregnations' of the past. Whatever is happening now is just an old story, an automatic effect of the overdetermined past. What we are experiencing today is nothing more than the product of the choices we made yesterday, and our inevitable 'choices' right now will determine our experiences tomorrow.

If a person believes that since they were not successful in business yesterday, they will not be successful today, change and movement is impossible. In this constricted, fatalistic understanding of time, the future is envisioned as already closed in front of us. We are not in a process of 'becoming' because we already 'became'. A person in this state of consciousness sees himself as a passive victim of the past.

YESH TIME & BEING PULLED BY AN UNDEFINED FUTURE

Another way of viewing linear time is that our present life is being pulled toward an undefined future. The future is yet to be, it has no predefined form or image, and thus we can imagine and become anything. We can let go of our past, and start over again, as every point of the future is an open horizon of infinite possibilities.

This state of perpetual 'becoming' is still part of a 'process' worldview, even though one is not being defined by their past. One is, rather, focused on dreams and hopes for the future, and on their drive to accomplish and create.

You are not a victim of your past, but rather an empowered creator of your life. The present moment is pregnant with unlimited potential; you can be what you want to be, now and in the future.

AYIN-TIME: EVERY MOMENT IS NEW

In a 'presence' paradigm or 'Ayin-time', the current moment is continuously appearing and arising fresh from no-thing-ness into consciousness and then instantaneously disappears again. There is no process of becoming, no lineage of influences, no real past or future, cause or effect. This model of time is, in a certain sense, cyclical; this moment is arising and vanishing over and over again, with no precedent or effect. There is no linear flow, and therefore past and future are but imaginary constructs. There is only the inescapable, infinite now.

Here is the paradox of this view. On the one hand, everything that exists exists in the now, and yet there is no such 'thing' as the now. This is experientially obvious: as soon as you become aware of the present moment, it has already passed. It is always 'here', but it's also always 'gone', having no duration. It is ungraspable, infinitely fluid, and fleeting in nature, it cannot serve as a container for separately existing events; nothing can be held by it. It is thus clear from this perspective that truly, *Ein Od Mil'vado* / "There is nothing but Infinite Divinity." Knowing this beyond a shadow of a doubt is the key to boundless freedom.

THE NEGATIVE ASPECT OF AYIN TIME

Ayin is actually more existent than all of existence; it is pure, alive Being. Nevertheless, it is possible to misunderstand Ayin, and Ayin-time, as 'nonbeing', the inert 'nothingness' of nihilism. One who falls into this negation of reality cannot change or grow, nor do they want to. They are only always here, now, neither pulled by a future nor birthed by a past. Deep down, they think there is no point or meaning to life, as nothing is really happening. If there is no time at all, a memory or a plan is just a fantasy. If there are no values, all laws are seemingly just forms of 'oppression'. While there is no anxiety and no regret in this state, there is also no creativity and no purpose to move forward. Nothing is important, and therefore there is zero motivation.

Even if one does not completely deny the existence of time, by attempting to reside permanently in the static peace of Ayin time, they can still lose all sense of drive. One can relax into non-judgmental witnessing and begin to think they are 'living in the now', but they are actually 'living *for* the now', and this is to be limited by the now. They may act with freedom and spontaneity but with no intentionality or consideration for the outcome of their actions. They discard responsibility for past actions and their consequences in the future.

'Living for the now' often takes the form of addictive or harmful eating and drinking and other acts of insatiability. Such an individual psychically shields themselves from the irony that they have become limited by their lack of limits, imprisoned by their freedom, and exclaims, 'Why not? You only live once, and all there is is right now. 'Good' and 'bad' are just thoughts!' They turn a blind eye to the ways they hurt themselves and others through their negative actions, excusing themselves with a claim that life is 'meaningless'.

Dwelling for a long time in this deceptively carefree state can eventually lead a person into *Yiush* / despondently giving up on life, to depression and lifelessness. This can lead further into unrestrained lust and risky behavior, as one develops, at least subconsciously, an increasingly dire need to feel alive in the face of the void they have constructed. At some point, they may do anything to gain a visceral sense of vitality, even if only for a couple of minutes. This is the shadow side of Ayin.

When time is imagined to be purely cyclical, and there is only the infinitely recurring present, there is no progress possible, nor meaningful goals or achievements. Everything is continually reset to zero; every movement reverts to stillness. An ever-repeating cycle without any linear element creates stagnation on all levels of self and society.

THE BENEFIT OF DIPPING INTO THE YESH & AYIN DIMENSIONS OF TIME

A dominant feature of our natural Yesh-world is development and progress. All of creation is in a constant state of flux and transformation, even something as seemingly still and dormant as a mountain. The nature and needs of our body and lower levels of our consciousness are like the rest of the natural world; they thrive on movement, progress, and success. Sitting idly brings boredom.

Passivity and stagnancy cause irritability, depression, self-loathing, and eventually energetic death.

Structured time, meeting challenges and goals, engaging in physical, mental, and spiritual exertion, actively extending kindness and love to others, attaining sustenance, and contributing to society, all keep the whole system vital and nourished. 'Yesh-time' benefits us, as it gives us a context in which to engage with all these life-giving processes.

Alternatively, when we are fully present in 'presence', nestled into the ever-unfolding formless moment, without superimposing labels or opinions, we are immersed in Ayin-time, which is actually timelessness.

Ultimately, we need both the release of Ayin-transcendence, as well as the generative resistance of Yesh-structure.

If we are exclusively bound to the paradigm of Yesh, we are either defined by our past and totally stuck — or we are pulled by desire, ambition, and perhaps anxiety about the future. If we are exclusively bound to the paradigm of Ayin, we will be so 'free' and detached that we will deny any connection to and responsibility for our past or our future. If we begin to only 'live for the now', we may eventually stumble into a stupor of lifelessness and depression. We need to untangle ourselves from overly identifying with the past or the future, but without becoming completely passive and living only for the moment.

How, then, can we derive the benefits of Yesh-time and of Ayin-timelessness, without getting stuck on either side?

One important strategy is called 'running and returning'. This involves remaining flexible enough to 'run' or shift into a state of timeless peace for periods of rejuvenation, and then to 'return' into the processes of structured time for periods of exertion, responsibility, and accountability.

Even a brief moment of dipping into timeless awareness is deeply refreshing, holistically healing — and long-lasting. For this reason, it is helpful to create a habit of briefly closing your eyes several times throughout the day, contacting the timeless witnessing presence within the stillness and peace at the base of experience. Rest there for a few moments throughout your day, and then return to your work or activity refreshed and alert.

Every time you feel weighed down by the Yesh of life, pause, settle your mind, deepen your presence, and attune yourself to the infinite 'weightlessness' of Ayin. Allow yourself to reset and start over.

It is also extremely beneficial to create or deepen a daily habit of mindfully reciting the affirmation of the Unity of the Divine, the *Shema*,* once in the morning and once in the evening (*for a transliteration and a spiritual translation of this chant, see the next section). You may pause to contemplate the meaning of the words, and use them as a gateway into timeless transparency. You can then pray from or meditate within this state of timeless unity, before going on to your daily activities or dinner or nighttime routine.

ESSENCE: THE ETERNAL MOMENT WITHIN THE FLOW OF TIME

Shema Yisrael, Ado-noy Elo-heinu; Ado-noy Echad....

Shema Yisrael / 'Listen Israel'

Ado-noy Elo-heinu / 'The Eternal, Infinite Timeless Ayin, is expressed and revealed, within Yesh, as the All-Powerful Force of Creativity...

(And yet,)

Ado-noy Echad / 'The Eternal, the unity of Ayin and Yesh, is always One'

Essence includes both Ayin and Yesh. 'Essence-time' unites timelessness and time in a way that brings out the best qualities of Ayin and the best qualities of Yesh, without detriment or contradiction. We can consciously exist within the eternally unfolding present moment even while following and harnessing the flow of linear process-time.

While the perspective of Yesh gives one room to wallow in regret, it also allows us to take responsibility for our past and to change its import for the future. This is the essence of *Teshuvah*, spiritual return, and ethical realignment. Yesh allows us to be 'in process' — to learn from our past mistakes, to grow and become wiser. Yet for change and growth to occur, it also requires the Ayin-timelessness paradigm, which is the basis for an empowering degree of freedom from the over-determined effects of the past.

When we make a mistake, in order not to be constrained by it, we need to be able to declare with confidence, 'This is a brand new moment! I can begin again, right now! I can choose a new, healthier, more loving path forward!' There is no past, there is no future, there is just endless potential for growth in this undefined, unstructured Ayin moment. This is the meaning of a Yiddish Chasidic song that has helped many generations of seekers overcome anxieties that limit positive action and wellbeing: "There is no yesterday, there is no tomorrow; all we have is 'a little bit of today' (this moment, right now), so why should we (get stuck in reactivity and) worry?"

In the essence of the present 'Ayin-Yesh' moment, there is no predetermined content and nothing that predicts an automatic future. Yet, paradoxically, this integral moment includes all of the past, future, and present in a way that is both deeply accountable and free from anxiety and despondency. The 'now' includes both Yesh and Ayin, action and stillness, time and timelessness. It is the larger context that includes being and becoming, process and presence. It is an infinite openness that supports the dynamism of life-giving action and structure. In 'Essence-time', we can truly 'live *in* the now,' rather than *'for* the now'.

LIVING IN THE EMPTINESS OF THE NOW

On a deeper level, living *in* the now means more than just being present with whatever is happening in this moment and witnessing the content flowing through our awareness. Living in the now can also mean being conscious of the emptiness and fullness of the experience, simultaneously. This could be called 'emptifullness'.

As an example of 'being present' in the essence-moment, we could take the activity of eating. As a practice, we would observe ourselves eating, remaining mindfully aware of everything that we are experiencing physically and psychologically during the process. We may take notice of the texture, temperature, and taste of every piece of food that is entering our mouth. We may also observe the play of our mood and emotions in response to the nourishment. On a spiritual level, we may also become mindful of the Source of the food by pausing before eating to say a blessing of gratitude over it.

Another eating practice can bring unconscious impatience or addiction-like craving and momentum up into the light of presence and awareness. This practice involves interrupting the mechanical act of mindlessly putting food in one's mouth. Pause between bites, place the fork or spoon back on the table and simply witness the thoughts, sensations, and emotions that arise, without reacting to them.

When you place the fork or spoon back on the table, your body may send a subtle signal of tension or anxiety, as if it is afraid it will be undernourished if not fed immediately. A subliminal narrative might also assert itself regarding a need for satisfaction or a demand for pleasing tastes. Let all of these feelings and narratives arise and recede for a few moments, and then notice also the undisturbed 'now'. Feel the peace of the infinite present. As a witness, you are not rushing toward any goal beyond attention. Feel the need for immediate gratification fade away as you immerse in the contentment of presence.

In this scenario, the deeper practice of being with 'emptifullness' in the moment is to become aware of the content, as above — and simultaneously the context, the space of the now itself, namely, the pure awareness in which the events are perceived to occur. Content and context, Yesh and Ayin, responsibility and detachment, are actually expressions of one inseparable essence.

Rather than merely dipping into Ayin-timelessness and then returning to dynamic action in Yesh-time, the way of essence is 'to be *and* not to be' at the same time. The content of awareness, whatever appears to our perception, is actually in no way separate from the awareness itself. For instance, without an awareness of a piece of food, it doesn't even appear before us. There is no 'seen' without a 'seer'. In the same way, there is no Yesh without Ayin. And the radical truth is that there is also no Ayin without Yesh. There is no stillness without reference to movement. Timelessness exists only in relation to time. The word 'timeless' itself hints at this fact, as it includes the word 'time'. Time and timelessness are essentially one.

All three aspects of time that we have discussed are expressed within the paradox of Essence-time: my past affects my present, my projected future affects my present, and my present is completely empty and still.

IN PRACTICAL LIFE

1. In paradigm one, the linear process of time moves unidirectionally from past to present. My past determines my present, and 'I am' but the cumulative effects of my past.

In this paradigm, I can own my past and take responsibility for it, but I still remain unavoidably defined by my past choices and experiences.

2. In paradigm two, in the linear process of time, the present is inexorably pulled from the future, I am drawn by my future, 'I am' a process of becoming. I do have a past, of course, but it does not define me. I am ambitious and forward-looking. So as not to be defined by my failures of the past, I will work even harder for my future.

In this paradigm, we might seek to break away from the past and envision for ourselves a brighter future. For instance, we might say, 'I will not be like my parents, who were not financially successful; I will work hard to build wealth.' True, we are refusing to be defined by our past, however, we are defined by how our past will not predict our future. In this way, not only our present, but even our future is determined by our past. Alternatively, in its purest form, paradigm two is completely positive, trustful, and inspirational, without needing to break away from, criticize, or even reference the past.

3. Paradigm three is pure presence, Ayin time, the boundless stillness of the moment. Deep in the background of daily experience, 'I am' pure presence and beingness, without any past or future. Due to this existential status at my root, I am always able to access the novelty and clarity of any particular moment and begin life anew, refreshed, unburdened, and unafraid — bringing this indomitable vitality into my activities and positive deeds in the world of time.

4. The fourth paradigm is not really a fourth, but an integral essence that includes and elevates all three perspectives as one.

"I am Yechidah, the Essence-soul; I raise up my past and my future, as well as my deeper timelessness, to their purely beneficial potency. I identify as a Yesh while remaining transparent to Ayin, giving me a lightness of being in the present moment, and empowering me to respond skillfully to my past and future.

With deep honesty, I take responsibility for my past, without being weighed down or defined by it. I am ambitious for my future, and I set courageous goals without being tied to a precise outcome or gain. I am content and in touch with a deeper stillness, quietness, and wholeness in the present moment, without becoming passive or dissociated from my responsibilities.

I choose to fully engage with life not because I would be anxious or depressed if I didn't, but rather just because I choose to. For example, I don't 'need' to make money ('need' implies a lack), rather I 'want' to work and earn because I want to house and support my family and give charity to good causes and those less fortunate. I am a timeless 'presence', living in the world of 'process' of my own volition. I am free."

How we experience time on a personal level, influences how we view and understand history in general. With this in mind, we will apply the paradigms developed above to larger cycles of historical time.

1) PARADIGM 1: BEING DEFINED BY THE PAST, VIEWING HISTORY WITH PESSIMISM

In this paradigm, where one's view is defined by the past, "nothing is new under the sun." History follows an ever-repeating pattern of birth, maturation, and death. A society may 'push a boulder up the mountain,' but that boulder will always roll down again, and will need to be pushed up the mountain again and again. There can be no real progress or human development. Civilizations emerge, flower for a while, then die. Another civilization comes to replace the previous one, but it will never be qualitatively better than what came before. People will always be essentially the same as they were in the past. Forms may change but the pattern remains the same; there is no real hope of the world ever becoming a better place.

Since the Enlightenment Period in Europe, it has become fashionable for intellectuals to uphold a banner of cynicism, nihilism, and pessimism, while hope and progress are left to naive romantic poets. The Existentialists who lived through the horror of the World Wars declared that our world is hopeless and all we can do is learn to live without hope. There are only questions, no answers. Morbid 'fate' reigns supreme.

As everything is just the effect of past influences, there is no possibility for personal growth or collective evolution. We and the world are stuck in a loop. The conditions into which a person is born, from their social status to their genetic makeup, from their astrological constellation to their 'personal interests', are all-determinative and forever fixed and sealed. In fact, there are no actual 'personal interests', for each person is no more than a culturally defined and predetermined expression of their past. This idea gave rise to "Philosophical Pessimism": life is basically meaningless and without purpose.

2) PARADIGM 2: BEING PULLED BY THE FUTURE, VIEWING HISTORY WITH PASSIVE OPTIMISM

A very different way of approaching history is with passive optimism: 'In the end, everything will work out.' History is, on its own, marching forward to a brighter future. An evolutionary process is embedded within Creation. Just as the various forms of life are evolving from simplicity to complexity, so too is mankind. We are always on an upswing. The present is inescapably being pulled by the future, and the future is inevitably brighter.

3) PARADIGM 3: AYIN-TIMELESSNESS, VIEWING HISTORY WITH INDIFFERENCE

Some have a worldview that is 'agnostic' regarding progress and regression. It is neither optimism nor pessimism. One remains uncertain about the trajectory of history, and therefore he drops out of the drama of life entirely. In certain 'privileged' sub-cultures, people may attempt to tune out and live with indifference to all the dramas of history. In this way, they can live, at least for some time, without a sense of anxiety. Yet this inner peace can breed indifference to the world around them. Indeed, an over-focus on asceticism and 'detached witness consciousness' can come at the expense of material development and a desire to solve real-world problems such as poverty, hunger, or illness.

Conversely, perhaps it is true that a great many of the world's major scientific and medical breakthroughs have occurred in societies steeped in a worldview of progress, ambition, and a strong sense of linear Yesh-time. However, that too often comes at the expense of more spiritual sensitivity, obstructing access to Ayin-time.

In the Torah, history begins with Creation and will ultimately culminate in Redemption. Some societies, throughout history, may have developed profound insights into 'presence', but in their cyclical world, there is no 'Genesis', no beginning, and thus no end or purpose, and thus no movement toward a worldwide redemption. If everything is cyclical and there is no origin or destination, why even bother to struggle for physical, economic, or societal change? Where the drama of life is seen as 'illusory', the ideal becomes dropping out of society, retreating into emptiness, and stepping off the wheel of life altogether.

On one level, it may be spiritually, emotionally, and psychologically healthy to retreat into presence-time, as we may reach a deep state of peace, focus, light, and spiritual pleasure. Yet without a 'beginning' or 'end', there is no ultimate purpose to being alive. And without a sense of purpose, that peace, focus, light, and spiritual pleasure cultivated in Ayin-time is never leveraged to alleviate the suffering of others. Within a dead-end world, no one has ever been substantially helped; an escapist has no interest in supporting others.

Mythology dominates this worldview. The basic premise of pagan mythology and its multiple, competing 'divinities', is an inevitable tragedy. Despite the intense dramas of each force attempting to outwit the other, any 'victory' is eventually forfeited, since, in the end, everything simply goes back to the way it was before. All the multiple (assumed) 'deities' (i.e., forces in the universe), such as the sun and other celestial spheres, are all warring with each other for control and dominance. Yet, there is a degree of inherent hierarchy between the numerous forces of nature, and so the cosmos as a whole is inevitably tragic, with each force vying to overcome its inherited lot, to no avail. Stasis reigns here. Despite all the ceaseless conflict and striving for power, in the end, everything always goes back to the 'way it was'. This is the law of eternal return.

Someone with this worldview will inevitably throw up their hands and claim that you can never make the world a better place; rather than waste your life trying, you should seek liberation from the world and cut ties with this realm. Indifference to others is reinforced because every 'accomplishment' is merely a copy of the cyclical past.

Mythology is an expression of a 'collective unconscious' expressed in symbolic forms. In a closed belief system of cyclical time and unconscious forces, life is seen as a closed system; as is one's relationship to life. Real change or progress is simply not possible in a closed system; there is no real possibility for transcendence. This is why, on a personal level, one may struggle against their nature, their environment, and predicaments, and perhaps be temporarily victorious, but at the end of the day, everything just reverts back to how it began. There is no 'linear' movement or progress, and so "the hero's journey" always ends tragically. From this perspective, life itself is indeed a great tragedy.

Greek tragedy is an aesthetic ritual that grew out of ancient mythology. In these dramas, the hero figure wishes to journey away from his assumed fate but is always bitterly disappointed. The Greeks believed in *moria* or *anake*, 'blind fate'; the idea that we can try to work against fate, but in the end, fate always wins. At birth, your life is already set. Some people may feel the urge to make a difference, to better themselves, or to do something beyond what is expected or accepted, but they inevitably grow old, lose their influence, and fade into oblivion. As the world is a fixed system, they fail to make any lasting difference. No breakthrough to a better life is possible.

In this ouroboric conception of the universe, there is no essential goodness in life, only an endless and inevitable cycle of struggle, tragedy, and death. You are doomed from the beginning; negative traits cannot be overcome; your genetics, your upbringing, and your social class dictate who you are and who you will be; your destiny is locked in. The world cannot get any worse, but nor can it get better; the only thing you can do is attempt to liberate yourself from this world and depart forever from this terrible realm.

All of these very real pitfalls emerge when one stays too long suspended in Ayin-time, and only serve to underscore the importance of the highest, deepest, and truest way of living, the way of Essence. Living with essence-time reveals and extracts the beneficial nature of both Ayin and Yesh, linear and cyclical time.

4) PARADIGM 4: ESSENCE-TIME, VIEWING HISTORY WITH PRACTICED OPTIMISM

In the view of 'essence-time', there is a notion of linear progress, as well as an eternal presence of all-inclusive unity: a oneness of Yesh and Ayin. Despite the appearance of increasing negativity, aggression, spiritual pollution, and material hardship in our times, it can be said that humanity is gradually learning from its mistakes and letting go of barbarism, idolatry, hopelessness, and moral depravity. More and more people are trading fatalistic and reactive thinking for deeper wisdom, understanding, compassion, and human nobility. We are spiraling toward redemption, the world of essential Divine unity.

As essence-time includes the linear model of Yesh-time, in this view, one is able to appreciate that history is continuously progressing. It is flowing from the primordial act of creation (past), traversing a period of struggle and clarification (present), and finally resolving in a great homecoming of all beings (future).

Many ancient peoples have perceived and celebrated the Presence of the Creator of Life within the natural world. They have thanked the Divine life force for the rain, the soil, and the cyclical harvest — blessings in the realm of physical matter or 'space'. Yet, the Torah reveals to us that the Divine Presence is also found in the linear flow of time and the trajectory of history. In fact, time was created as the foundation of space.

How do we consciously receive and celebrate the blessings of time? There are different positive potentials embedded in the three paradigms of time, as explored earlier. 1) As life moves from past to present, we can change our habits and heal our past, transforming the outcome of our mistakes into blessings. 2) The more optimistic view, that life in the present is being pulled by a brighter, yet undefined future, is itself a blessing. The present is thus influenced by a better future. 3) As we gain the ability to be present with the timeless backdrop and context of time, we become still and equanimous and able to begin anew at every moment, without anything to change or await. There has never been anything but blessing.

The way of essence unites all three of these paradigms. We can change the trajectory of our past, we can allow the redemptive culmination of history to illuminate our present by drawing the light of the future (*Chayei HaOlam HaBa* / the Life of the World to Come) into our present consciousness, and we can know and feel that there is nothing other than redemption here and now, without becoming passive or insensitive.

We will not blame ourselves for our past; we will effortlessly accept responsibility for it and be free of all negativity. We will not just sit back and wait passively for a brighter future but rather participate in its unfolding. We will enter the timeless presence of redemption and perfection without losing touch with the process of time and all its challenges. In this way we will live from a place of radical trust in the Higher Power as we go about becoming an agent of redemption.

As essence, we are the blessing and the change that we want to see. Just as we can change, we can effect change. As such, our optimism is not passive, nor laced with anxiety or indifference; nor is our optimism driven by hubris or spiritual ego, as if we were some great saviors, bearing the answers to every question. Here, hope is not a mere ideology, but an activity; being practically engaged, selflessly yet confidently, bringing positive change to everyone around us.

To believe that we can make a difference necessitates deep faith in ourselves. Indeed, as the wise ones have said, "Even faith needs faith." We need to believe that the future will be bright, and yet still do everything in our power to make it happen. In this way, essence-time is far more transformative and manifests far greater benefits than all the positive potentials of all three modes, combined. It is a whole greater than the sum of its parts.

TRANSFORM YOURSELF AND TRANSFORM THE WORLD

Rebbe Moshe of Sasov, a 19th-century mystical master, once said: "As a young man, I thought I would change the world, but the world did not change. When I grew a little older, I decided to change the people of my town, but that, too, didn't happen. When I got married and had a family, I decided to change them, but to no avail. Then I realized, I must first transform myself! And the truth is, if I change myself, I will naturally change my family, my town, and the world."

Today we understand that measuring a subatomic particle in one location may instantaneously affect the measurement of another particle thousands of miles away. This is referred to as 'quantum entanglement'. Two particles that have previously been in contact become deeply 'entangled' or interconnected. When they are then separated, they can 'communicate' faster than light, a change in one prompting a virtually simultaneous change in the other. This phenomenon does not diminish with distance. Such 'quantum non-locality' has been tested experimentally for a few decades.

The ability of birds to locate their home from thousands of miles away may be associated with such non-local quantum phenomena. The interconnected nature of the universe is further confirmed with regard to animal behavior. Studies have been performed demonstrating that the behavior of one particular animal affects the behavior of the entire species. When a group of rats, for example, were trained to execute a task in one lab across the globe, it was reported that rats of the same breed in other labs learned that same task more quickly. Apparently, the first group had somehow influenced the second group, despite their great distance.

Notwithstanding the ever-changing nature of scientific findings and theories, this idea of 'quantum non-locality' is a good metaphor for how your singular consciousness affects the consciousness of the entire world. Any 'micro-consciousness' has a bearing on the 'macro-consciousness'. On some level, our state of mind is projected into the ether, so to speak, and engenders a subtle shift in reality as a whole. When we transform a part, we transform the whole.

THE MORE HOPE WE HAVE, THE MORE HOPE THE WORLD WILL HAVE

If we live with hope, we release a positive resonance, as it were, into the world. Through our individual attainment of hope, the quality of the spiritual and emotional 'oxygen' in the world chang-es, and people in different locations around the world can 'breathe in' more hope. Hope breeds hope; when people start living with a greater sense of hopefulness, they feel more empowered to change the world, and they become engaged in acts that change the world for the better, thus giving others more hope.

We cannot fight against pessimism and hopelessness when we see others in a cynical light. We may perceive that people have become so overstimulated by contemporary lifestyles that they have collapsed into moral indifference or confusion. We may view ourselves as exceptionally passionate for change, full of faith, hope, wonder, and commitment, while we judge our family and friends as being uninterested or non-committal, lacking all hope. How-ever, such judgments block our ability to connect to and influence others, revealing a gap in our own faith. We need faith in faith, and hope regarding hope; believing deeply that others have faith and hope deep within them, that they too have the Divine Image within them, a living spark of wholeness and perfection. That point of shared connection is a medium through which our signals can be transmitted. Our positive states and actions create waves that are picked up by our friends, family members, community, and world; and we, in turn, are open to receive from them as well.

Here is a mystical tale that is told about one of the greatest scholars of law, Rebbe Yoseph Caro, and one of the greatest mystics and Kabbalists in all of history, Rebbe Yitzchak Luria, known as the Arizal.

Rebbe Yoseph Caro once labored long over a difficult question on the Talmud, when one night, a solution finally came to him. The next day in his academy, as he was just about to deliver a lecture presenting his newfound insight, one of his students asked if he could first attempt to decipher the text. To his amazement, the student offered the exact interpretation that he was about to share. Later that day, the stunned sage chanced upon his contemporary, the Arizal, and told him of the event. The Arizal explained: 'In truth, it was you who brought this insight down into the world. But once it was here, it became accessible to all, and your student tapped into it.'

Once something has already been done it is easier to repeat it. Some theorists have called this phenomenon "formative causation" or "morphic resonance." One of the illustrations cited by these theorists is a study in which subjects were presented with three poems in Japanese transliteration. One was a well-known Japanese poem, another was a string of random Japanese words, and the third was a newly composed poem. All of the subjects were men who were unable to understand Japanese. Interestingly, they found it much easier to memorize the well-known poem than the other two, despite the fact that they had no idea what the words meant.

If we can activate and establish within ourselves positive and elevated states of consciousness, it will become easier for others around the world to do the same. The more positivity and elevation we generate within our lives and relationships, the more positivity and elevation spreads throughout the very fabric of this universe, and the more people become susceptible to experiencing the hope of redemption. The more hope we have the more hope others will have, and the more hope there will be for the world.

CULTURE VIRUSES

On the flip side of "morphic resonance," negativity breeds negativity. A 'culture virus' can form when specific negative patterns of behavior are perpetuated in one area of the globe. If, somehow, these behaviors catch on and become contagious, people around the world may begin to act in the same way. For example, without even seeing images or hearing it discussed, young people in one location can begin engaging in the same destructive behavior as their peers in another, distant location. For example — may the Compassionate One prevent it — when there was a spike in kids harming themselves in a particular way in one place, kids in other locations around the world 'spontaneously' replicated it. If this can happen with harmful acts, certainly it can also happen with beneficial acts. In fact, "morphic resonance" can be harnessed for positivity and greater well-being on a much wider scale, since positivity creates a generative 'feedback loop'; our inspiration and faith influences others to have inspiration and faith as well.

Positivity is inherently more powerful than negativity; the very nature of life-affirming faith and hope is to self-propagate and multiply. Our positivity is particularly contagious when our striving for progress is coupled with the inner peace of 'presence'. This is because, deep down, everyone wants success and to have the ability to help others and change the world for the better, all while feeling deep satisfaction within.

When we combine the responsibility and drive of process and Yesh-time with the peace and contentment of presence and

Ayin-timelessness, we become full to overflowing with hope and trust in the Divine plan. Moreover, this hope is not tied to any set outcome. For example, if we are involved in a certain project and we hope for its success, even if it falls apart completely, we will be able to get up and try again or try something new. In any case, we will not become defeated or dispirited, or give up trying. Hope, coupled with inner contentment, gives us the ability to always get up after a failure. Even if our hope has been dashed, we can joyfully start over again with the same vitality and vigor as if it were the first time.

Highly positive people naturally have a sense that there is a greater plan playing out, that the Creator runs the world with Perfect Wisdom and we are but partners, co-creators in the un-folding of events. True, we need to do our part and be dependable partners by being independent thinkers and dreamers, maintaining steadfast faith and tremendous hope in a brighter tomorrow, and actively working to create that future. In fact, the 'vessel' that most productively draws down Divine light and flow into experience is this very hope and positive expectation. Yet, if we do not see the fruition of our hopes, we should not become despondent and lose faith; we are simply being called to dig within for a deeper hope.

Ultimately, our soul knows that there is a greater plan unfolding; sometimes we consciously see the fulfillment, and sometimes we don't, but deep down, we intuit that the fulfillment is coming; and deeper still, that it is, was, and will be, always already right here and right now.

Living in 'process-time' means looking toward the future, hoping it will be good. Presence-mind is having radical acceptance of 'what is' right now, whatever the situation. The unity of process-time and timeless presence is 'essence-time'.

In this unified state, we draw fruit of the future into the seed of the present, manifesting redemption even within exile.

03

PROCESS & PRESENCE WITHIN RELATIONSHIPS:
MASCULINE AND FEMININE QUALITIES

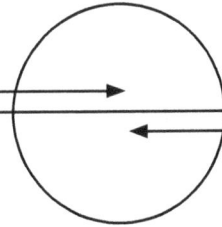

P ROCESS AND PRESENCE ARE REFLECTED IN ALL DYNAMICS OF life, including in our interpersonal relationships. When we understand these dynamics more deeply, we can resolve conflicts and bring blessings to those we love.

There is the dynamic of the 'giver', which is termed 'masculine'. This is expressed in forward or outward-facing proactive movement, and is often experienced as assertiveness, extraversion, ambition, and 'process'. There is also the dynamic of the 'receiver', termed 'feminine'. This is expressed in inward movement, and experienced as receptivity, introspection, hiddenness, and 'presence'.

Each of us has a combination of these two qualities, in a balance that is unique to us. Some of these different capacities are hardwired into the nature of our biologies, and perhaps some may have to do with nurture and socialization; however, these two basic behavioral patterns are imprinted and enacted by all humans in numerous ways. Familiarizing ourselves with their inner dynamics provides us with fresh insight into various character types, including our own, allowing human relationships to more consciously flourish.

GOAL-ORIENTED OR RELATIONSHIP-ORIENTED

Femininity is also called *Malchus* (or *Malchut*) / royalty, human nobility, the majesty of things as they are, and inwardness. Malchus seeks to share nobility by creating healthy relationships and trustworthy friendships. A person with this quality thinks in terms of caretaking and nurturing, cultivating community and holding presence.

Masculinity, also called Yesod, is outwardly oriented, always seeking solutions to challenges and working to reach goals. In these ways, it is 'process' and goal-oriented. A person with this quality thinks in terms of achievements and gains.

While Yesod sets its sights on a destination, Malchus recognizes the beauty and presence of the journey itself. To understand this on a practical level, try the following experiment. As you are walking on the way to work or an appointment, be conscious and aware of what you are walking towards. Are you mainly trying to get to your destination, from point A to point Z, or do you have an interest in the walk itself? Is walking just a means to an end, or could there be a purpose simply in walking? When you are present with the walk itself, with what you're seeing and feeling, and with the miraculous life-force that allows you to put one foot in front of the other, how does the nature of the journey change?

Orientations of 'process' and 'presence' are at play in many areas of life, including the ways we communicate. When faced with a challenge, someone inhabiting the feminine quality of Malchus may seek to simply describe the problem to an empathetic listener. Indeed, to be 'present with the journey' in this way can be even more important than communicating with the goal of determining a solution. Just knowing that you are being heard can often resolve the sense of difficulty or any anguish and anxiety in the challenge that you are facing.

Someone inhabiting the masculine quality of Yesod may be inclined to seek help to find a *practical* solution to a problem. If a male is deeply entrenched in this perspective (as males generally are), it will be difficult for him to listen to a female who just wants to be heard as she describes a challenge. He may attempt to offer an unwanted solution, and then become surprised when she doesn't accept the resolution but rather continues to explain the challenge. She is focusing on the journey while he is focusing on the destination. This can frustrate both parties.

ALL OF US CONTAIN BOTH

Related to their spiritual roots, women and men generally have very different communication styles. For example, women often find comfort in speaking to others more than men do. On some level, we all have both feminine and masculine qualities within us, and we need to exercise both and balance these traits. A masculine trait of goal orientation, when not checked by the corresponding feminine trait of connection, can lead to impatience and an inability to learn from mistakes. A feminine trait of sympathy, when not checked by the corresponding masculine trait of competition, can lead a person to become oversensitive and indecisive. All people need both traits and to exercise them in balance. We need to cultivate the skill of nurturing, listening, and sharing presence, as well as the skill of inspiring decisiveness and striving resolutely to attain a goal.

Health, whether biological, psychological, or spiritual, is a condition of balance and harmony. For example, when our conscious, rational self comes to terms with our unconscious layers of self, the dynamics of presence and process are reconciled and harmonized within a greater wholeness. This allows us to live with more ease and less tension.

CIRCLES & LINES

Masculine souls, who principally incarnate into male bodies, are rooted in a meta-physical inner world called *Kav* / 'Cosmic Line'. Feminine souls, who principally incarnate into female bodies, are rooted in the inner world called *Igul* / 'Cosmic Circle'. The line and the circle are also reflected in the physical anatomy, and in the feminine life cycles.

Goal-oriented living expresses a linear paradigm, and presence-oriented living reflects a circle paradigm. Physicality and empirical observations and truths are connected with the 'linear' reality, while the inner world of spirituality and intuitive truths are rooted in the world of 'circular' reality.

Lines are defined; there are directions such as up and down, earlier and later. Circles have no beginning or end. To the eye, a point on a circle does not have a fixed, identifiable location, unless the circle is placed in the context of a grid of *lines* that indicate up and down, left and right, north-south and east-west, etc. The world of circles is thus a world of undefinable, flexible, and timeless presence.

MEN & WOMEN

Obviously, there are exceptions to every pattern, and every rule has exceptions, but to better understand the difference and distinctions between 'line' and 'circle' paradigms as manifest within human traits and behaviors, we will resort to some sweeping generalizations.

Spiritual sensitivity, faith, faithfulness, and a desire for commitment, can often be found more in women than in men. Insofar as men are programmed and built for physical conquest, they tend to be more aggressive, and hence more inclined to promiscuity.

They see others in the context of their own 'linear' goals, and once the goal has been accomplished, the relationship can be deprioritized. Women see others in terms of wholeness, completeness, and the circle of 'eternal' commitment.

A businessman tends to see the CEO of another company in one dimension: he is a competitor. He may even be seen abstractly as 'competition'. A businesswoman, by contrast, may see that same CEO as a real person with a spouse, a person with parents, with children, with feelings and needs. She can sometimes see the full 360-degree panorama (circle) of a person, while a man is focusing on a certain trajectory or outcome (line).

Insofar as women want affirmation and acknowledgment, when a husband remembers a milestone in the relationship, this can stand out for her more than an expensive gift given without sentimentality. For a man, a valuable gift may stand out more than a sentimental gesture.

Men seek 'progress' while women seek 'unity'. In spiritual pursuits, men often seek elevation and gain, while women seek integration and ways of giving. In terms of social standing, males climb vertically, while females expand horizontally in circles of inclusion or withdraw into circles of protection.

DIFFERENT FORMS OF RELATIONSHIP

A line implies exclusivity; there are leaders and followers with different privileges and a strong sense of one-way communication. In a circle, everyone has a place; no one is a head or a tail. Each point in a circle is equal, each connected with all others, communicating and communing. Everyone is seen and valued; children, the elderly, and the infirm all have something to contribute.

BENEFITS AND PITFALLS OF THE DIFFERENT RELATIONSHIP STYLES

These dual dynamics play out, particularly in the understanding of the basic purpose of a relationship. In the masculine mode, a relationship often serves an external objective or 'process'. A relationship can more often be an alliance for mutual gain or a contract in which one is benefitting or serving the other. A man may make a friend when he perceives it will help him gain information, wisdom, notoriety, honor, or financial advantages. To a greater or lesser extent, his interest is in his linear mobility in the world. A pitfall can easily form in this mode of relationship if profits become the sole motivation and 'process' eclipses 'presence' and personal warmth.

In the feminine mode, the purpose of a relationship can be in the relationship itself. One can be present with people just for the sake of 'presence'. Relationships are about sharing thoughts and feelings and being there for others. No person is regarded as a means to an end. Yet, a pitfall can form in this mode of relationship if one partner becomes overly dependent on the other's empathy and all 'linear' individuality is erased.

We all need and crave genuine presence with others, not just profitable alliances. Yet, it can also benefit everyone to not 'need' to be relating to others at all times, and certainly not to base our self-esteem on the warmth of others.

How can we include the benefits of masculine process and feminine presence in our relationships, while avoiding the pitfalls that each presents? The balance between goal-oriented interactions and empathetic presence with others will look different for different people. We can express a need for empathy without demanding it from others. We can benefit from alliances without using them as objects. There may be strangers in our environment whom we should not pour out our heart to, and there are certainly people close to us whom we should not view as potential sources of profit.

Healthy love is unconditional. Conditional love stems from need, and it will always want something, whether that is utilitarian gain or empathetic warmth. It will never be satisfied, because enforcing 'love' or grasping for 'love' incites an ever-deepening sense of lack.

Giving love unconditionally creates self-sufficiency in the giver. A partner who gives because he or she "needs" something is not self-sufficient as an individual, and their lack of independence can become suffocating to their partner. Conversely, couples who have a higher "want" for each other, a drive to share life with the other, feel whole in themselves individually, and also feel supported by the relationship.

Immature love says, 'I am nobody without you; I need you.' This is a posture of taking. When people feel neediness from others, they recoil. Mature love says, 'I can stand on my own, and yet I am choosing to love you.' The desire for the relationship thus comes from a place of 'want' and not from a place of 'need'. This is a posture of true giving; when people feel 'wanted', they feel honored and tend to reciprocate the honor.

THE PATH OF ESSENCE IN RELATIONSHIPS

The classic path of creating an essential unity of masculine and feminine is the path of marriage. With the unifying force of a covenant, an indelible commitment between souls, masculine and feminine qualities are able to reconcile while remaining distinct, and the relationship can become "an eternal structure."

Adam and Chavah / Eve are the prototypes of male and female marriage partners. The Torah narrative tells us that Chavah was created as a "helper against him." On one level, this means that one partner can either "help" their spouse or work "against" their spouse, depending on how both partners relate to one another vis-a-vis process and presence. This dynamic may be especially pertinent to 'Chavah', the wife, but it can apply to whoever is playing the role of 'nurturer' in the relationship. A husband trying to help his wife manifest her gifts and accomplish her life's mission, could unwittingly work "against" her or stand in her way.

In some relationships, both parties share many common interests, activities, and approaches to life. Rather than balancing each other out through tension and resolution, partners reflect and reinforce each other's energies by 'mirroring' each other. Both partners may have sought to unite with someone who was 'created in their own image', so to speak. The relationship is characterized by the partners peacefully supporting each other — 'helping' without the tension of being 'against' the other. On the surface, this type of relationship may be less challenging or more peaceful, although it may also be less dynamic and passionate.

TENSEGRITY IN RELATIONSHIP

Tensegrity is a condition of structural integrity that comes from a combination of surrounding or 'circular' interconnections and opposing linear tensions. In this type of relationship, two or more objects can be connected in an 'embrace', while remaining independent. Each object paradoxically 'helps' the other stabilize by pulling against it.

This metaphor will help us decipher the deeper meaning of "helper against him." Another translation of "against" is 'opposite'. A partner becomes a 'helper' precisely by being an 'opposite', a counter-balance to the other's traits and communication style. By challenging and even lovingly opposing each other, we "help" each other. The tension of opposing worldviews and dynamics creates a sense of chaos that forces each partner to respond from their higher self. This stimulates and reinforces greater mutual growth, order, and unification.

By providing each other with a countervailing force to wrestle with and then eventually align with, each partner is also able to highlight and call forth the unique talents of the other. In this tensegrity, each also illuminates the darker areas in which the other partner needs encouragement in order to become the best person they can be. In this way, a couple can both mirror *and* oppose one another, bringing together presence and process. While each partner sees their own beauty and perfection (presence) mirrored in the other, each is simultaneously shown where they can grow (process).

Yet, this requires tremendous sensitivity because often, the trait that you think your partner needs to 'fix' is the very trait that is meant to cause *you* to grow. The solution is to focus *only* on what you need to fix in yourself, never on what the other needs to fix in themselves. This is the 'integrity' within the 'tensegrity' of a healthy relationship.

THE PLACE OF GREATNESS IS THE PLACE OF FAULT

Often, a person's 'character flaw' is also their point of charm or source of their greatness. Indeed, sometimes what you do not like in your spouse may be directly related to what draws you to them. The following is an exercise that can help you harness any 'tension' toward increasing your 'integrity' in the way you relate to your significant other.

Think about three habits of your spouse that irritate you a little. For example, 1) he is disorganized, 2) he speaks excitedly and 'too loudly', and 3) he makes decisions without thinking. Now, think about three things you love about your spouse. Perhaps they correspond: 1) he is spontaneous, 2) he is full of life, and 3) he gets things done. His so-called faults are directly linked to his strengths. In other words, the ways he is 'against' you are directly linked to the ways he 'helps' you.

THE THIRD THAT COMES TO RECONCILE THE TWO

"Two opposite approaches clash one with one another until a 'third' comes to reconcile them." When a circle and a line reconcile, combine, and harmonize, they form a spiral. This represents the 'third' that comes to reconcile the two opposites. There is feminine presence *with* the masculine process, help *through* opposition, and achievement *with* communion. This is a tensegrity; connection *with* healthy distance, being drawn together while remaining on one's own feet as individuals, helping and opposing. When two separate people come together in unity — as 'two' and as 'one' — they will hopefully produce a 'third': a child. Often, a child will adopt and develop the best character traits of each parent. When this is so, each new generation brings that family tree, and the whole world, closer to redemptive perfection.

04

PROCESS & PRESENCE IN OUR OUTER WORK:

MEANS AND ENDS

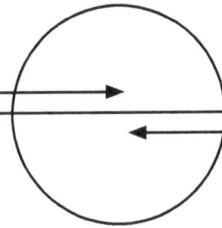

INNATE TO THE HUMAN BEING IS A NEED TO REST AND TRANSCEND the world. We all have a desire to let go of tension and live in spiritual bliss, yet, we also have a strongly ingrained desire to create, participate, innovate, and work. Thus, "The nature of the human being is to toil."

Although we are created beings, we are designed in the Image of the Creator, meaning, we are hardwired with a 'creator gene', an inexhaustible yearning for creativity, to be a creator in life. Deep down, we do not want to reap the benefits of others' hard work, but rather to participate in creating our sustenance. Even more profoundly, we desire to bestow benefits on our community and world.

Working and cultivating a sense of accomplishment are essential human needs, and they keep us awake and alert. To contribute to the greater good is part of who we are. We are creators just as much as we are creations.

Yet, beneath all the Yesh and noise / drama of the world, beneath all the ambition and effort of human toil, there is an inner stillness, an *Ayin* / emptiness, a perfect silence that we also uncover in moments of deep introspection, prayer, or contemplation. When we turn our attention away from thought and sense perception, we discover an effortless witnessing of life unfolding, a peaceful back-drop of all the drama. Here, everything is perceived as ever-perfect and whole. In this state of presence, it appears there is no work to be done; life is already as it is meant to be.

MEANS TO AN END

In the world of process, all activities are means to an end, even when that end remains forever elusive. For example, a person studies building so that she can build a home, so that she can live in the home. She lives in a home so that she can sleep well, so that she can have the strength during the day to study and build things. A person labors in a factory so that he can obtain enough money to buy food and take a little time to eat it, so that he will have the strength to go back to his labor. A little money will be left over to feed his children, so they can grow up and do the same.

In this way of life, you are never truly present with what you are engaged in, because a significant part of your mind and energy is focused on the future goal, the end. Presence is relegated to a future that never arrives.

EVERYTHING HAS VALUE IN ITSELF

A third approach to life is to engage in the challenging world of process, of becoming, of painstaking efforts to create a better reality — yet, at the same time to be consciously rooted in a state of pure being and presence. It is possible to enter the noisy marketplace without leaving the silent temple of inner awareness; and to engage in a broken world while remaining whole.

The great spiritual master, healer, and founder of Chasidic mysticism, the Baal Shem Tov, said, "When I was younger, I was in a state of pure awareness and *Deveikus* / unity with the Divine Presence. Yet, whenever I stepped outside, I felt that others would distract me and pull me out of my inner state. Only as I grew older I was able to remain in a state of Deveikus even among other people and their dramas." Revealing this level of 'unity in engagement', the Baal Shem Tov empowered us to do so as well: everyone, on their own level, can be simultaneously above and within the drama of life.

Living this way, all our movements are infused with stillness, purpose, and meaning. There is full presence with every action, as well as a recognition of the goal of the action. Everything we do has value; nothing is a mere means to an end. Even when a task is a step in a larger process, we have a sense of presence in that activity. When walking to the store, for example, we are fully conscious of walking. Experienced from a state of presence, the process of walking is actually quite miraculous — all the coordination, suspension, and balance, the muscles firing at exactly the right moment and angle to catch the next footfall.

Likewise, we can be conscious of *how* we are witnessing these events, including how our awareness seems to divide into a separate subject and object in order to "have" the experience. This can be called 'apperception', or 'watching the watcher'. To marry the pure witness with decisive action in daily life is to marry heaven and earth. This is what the mystics have called 'making *Yichudim* / unifications', or revealing the underlying essential unity of experience.

THE END IN THE MEANS

Creation has an end goal: the revelation of the Divine Unity underlying all the multiplicity of Creation. Striving for this redemption occurs in the world of movement. And yet, to 'accomplish' it, we must simultaneously enter, today, the stillness of Unity, where the 'end' is always already present within every detail of the 'means'.

Our presence is in our process, and our process *is* our presence. The 'end' is already present within the means. Formless presence is revealed within the procession of forms. And 'revealed' is an important term here — we are not actually 'making' this Unification come about. It is already the case, it is just not widely appreciated or noticed. All we really need to 'do' is to open our eyes to the reality of redemption.

LIVING, NOT 'THINKING' ABOUT LIVING

It should be pointed out that 'revealing' Unity in the multiplicity of our life does not simply mean 'thinking' about it. Just as it doesn't help to overlay our state of presence with thoughts about its purpose, overlaying our purposeful action with thoughts of presence and Unity is just another distraction. Rather than thinking *about* what you are doing or thinking *about* the underlying Unity, just *be* physically, emotionally, mentally, and spiritually present with experience — look directly at the unity of awareness and action as it is.

When a person is fully alive — not just physically breathing, eating, drinking, and procreating, but doing all these activities in connection with the Divine mandates of the Torah (the revelation of the Oneness of the Creator), then they are living the 'end' *within* the means, drawing the perfect unity of the World to Come into the now.

Life itself is the purpose of life — to be truly and authentically alive on all levels of our being; physically, emotionally, mentally, spiritually, and wholly.

When we 'make unifications', or reveal the Divine Unity of presence and process in everything we do, we are revealing the goal of Creation in every moment.

Living in this way opens our eyes to a most awesome and profound awareness.

We recognize that the most important time in history is now.

The most important place in the world is right here.

The most important person in the human race is you.

The most important thing that can be done in this most important time and place by the most important person, is the very thing you are doing where you are, right now.

Experiencing life through this lens is to kindle and bask in the *Ohr* / Light of *Geulah* / redemption within us, right here and right now.

05

PROCESS & PRESENCE IN OUR INNER WORK:
IMPERFECTION AND PERFECTION

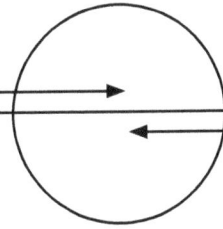

J UST AS THERE ARE PHYSICAL ACTIVITIES WE MUST DO TO physically survive and thrive, there are inner spiritual, intellectual, and emotional processes that we need to actively engage in order to thrive at our highest level. As people mature, many evolve from wanting merely to survive to wanting to thrive, physically. Then they may break through into wanting to thrive on the deeper levels of their being. First, they try to secure some measure of physical and economic security, and once their basic existential needs are taken care of, they may begin to think more about their need for love, knowledge, personal growth, character refinement, and connection. This is a natural and organic progression from physical advancement to emotional and intellectual refinement, to spiritual expansiveness.

Having achieved some sense of spiritual transcendence, some people consider working on their character traits to be of lesser importance: 'I am becoming deeply still and illumined; why should I go backward and worry about my unrefined behavioral patterns?' However, spiritual pursuits need to be tied to positive development of our character traits, as clarified character traits are actually the foundation of true spiritual growth. In fact, the inner spiritual work we do in our private relationship with the Creator is actually rooted in, and proven by, our skillful and generous relationships with others.

In fact, as the Rebbe Rayatz, the great Chassidic Master of the previous generation, teaches, the very purpose of all spiritual and inner work is to transform the nature of our character traits. To achieve this, every day, we should spend at least a few minutes studying and meditating upon positive character traits such as compassion, judging others favorably, being patient, showing respect, cleanliness, forgiveness, honesty, modesty, thoughtfulness, and joy.

LAYERS OF DEPTH WITHIN US

Our 'revealed' levels of self are those that we show to the world, in the ways we act and speak. We also have 'concealed' levels of self, which can be very different from the ways we express and externally manifest ourselves in the world. A person can harbor private thoughts that are the opposite of their public appearance or even of their own self-image. Hopefully, our subconscious mind is vibrant, positive, holy, and noble. But even if this is so, within more 'subterranean' or subconscious dimensions, there can be a cold darkness, with unresolved traumas or unfulfilled primal desires that can bubble up into the mind as errant thoughts or perverse longings.

Yet, deeper still, beneath all the layers of revealed light and hidden darkness, deeper than our muddied or opaque subconscious, is our essential soul. We might need to dig beneath a layer of vegetation and life-giving soil, and even beneath a layer of cold, lifeless stone, in order to uncover a treasure of diamonds. Yet, at our deepest core, there is gem-like perfection and indissoluble wholeness.

We have three major layers of self: 1) our surface identity, the self we project outwardly to the world, 2) a deeper identity that is known only to us, which may only be experienced when we are alone, and 3) the diamond essence of our soul, a shimmering shard of the Divine, which never changes despite our private feelings and failings. This essential wholeness perpetually pushes us to be our best self, and to unify all levels of our being.

OUR THREE NAMES

We all have three 'names': 1) the name that our parents called us; 2) the 'name' that we call ourselves, meaning our private, hidden identity; and 3) the name the Creator called us before we came into this world.

We each have a choice regarding which of these three names will become our primary identity: "the name that we acquire through our choices and actions."

The name that other people call us is usually related to the name our parents gave us. This is, in a sense, the name of our 'body' and projected self. But we also have another name, the identity that only we know; the private 'name' that calls upon the characteristics of our subconscious mind. If we are an inwardly confident, happy, optimistic person by nature, we can "acquire" this name, and identify primarily with wholeness, even outwardly.

Sadly, many people project confidence and happiness outwardly, but their inner name and private identity is riddled with insecurity, conflict, and despondency. Even many outwardly 'successful' people — thriving financially, socially, and intellectually — when alone with themselves, feel like imposters. If their success is tied to material possessions, physical beauty, or social status, they are always worried that they do not deserve what they have, and that they could lose everything at any moment. Deeper than this insecurity is a layer of the subconscious mind which can also be fractured or deadened by unmet needs and the buried traumas of life. One might also 'acquire' this chaos and brokenness as their primary identity if his or her choices are unwise and reactive.

Yet underneath all of these layers of experience shines our innate essence, which roots and pushes us to be who we are meant to be in the world. It is like the DNA in the seed of an apple tree, the Divine intelligence that informs its growth and pushes it through all the resistance of the rocky substratum, the ever-changing soil conditions, and weather events, to be the best apple tree possible. This is the name that the Creator of All Life gives us before we are born. It is the name that pushes us to be our best self, no matter the outer and inner conditions in which we find ourselves.

NOTICE WHERE YOU ARE CHALLENGED

In the 'outer world' of words and actions, we all need to train ourselves to speak more kindly and mindfully, and to act more intentionally and less reactively. In order to achieve any type of spiritual well-being, we need to struggle consistently to refine ourselves; it doesn't just come naturally.

To traverse this path, we must become aware of the ways in which we need to grow, and where we are broken, flawed, and unwhole. Life itself guides us in this process if we merely pay attention. We are shown what we need to refine based on our experiences of fear, anger, despondency, and insatiable desire. For example, we may ask ourselves, what is the most difficult *Mitzvah* / Torah-imbued action for me to do? What do I find to be the most challenging positive action or the one that brings up the most inner resistance for me? This action is a vital part of our spiritual calling in life.

INNER WORK ON THE LEVEL OF PROCESS: 'BREAKING COMPULSIONS'

One common difficult growing point for people is the challenge of physical compulsions or lusts and a painful sense of insatiability. The inner work of breaking cravings, compulsions, and self-defeating patterns of behavior is called *Iskafya* / 'refraining', reconditioning the body and mind through interrupting unwanted behavior patterns. Whenever some desire for fulfilling a negative urge rises up, you firmly push it away as many times as necessary and then take care of the authentic underlying need. One way to push it away is to get up abruptly and go get absorbed in something healthy, or at least harmless, that you enjoy.

For example, if you find yourself alone, compulsively eating an entire container of ice cream, stop, and tell yourself that you will just temporarily delay eating it. Meanwhile, put it away and leave the area. Go immediately to get some exercise, talk with a friend, get some sun, or leave the building.

Once you have fully distracted yourself and you are removed from the situation, then you can sit down and feel the sensations and emotions associated with the compulsion. If you can stay with uncomfortable bodily energies without reaction or tension, they will fade. Doing this in the presence of another person is helpful, in case you are drawn back into the behavior. If and when you feel pulled to eat too much ice cream again, you can actively deter yourself by first pouring ketchup or salt and pepper on it, or something that decreases or nullifies your attraction to it.

Most importantly, examine the source of the compulsion, the authentic, adaptive need beneath it. Does a nutritional deficiency, lack of sleep, or an underlying sense of anger or sadness drive the behavior? What can you do to meet your needs for physical and emotional health?

Responding compassionately to these real needs will help you break your desires more than 'asceticism' will. Countless 'normal' people have used this process of Iskafya successfully; you don't have to be an outstanding spiritual adept to do it. If a compulsion is stubborn or recurring, don't give up; continue your inner work. Consult a trusted mentor as well, someone you can be honest with and who can help you stay accountable to self-compassion and growth.

WHY THE STRUGGLE & PROCESS?

One might ask, why go through the trouble and effort of interrupting compulsions and refining character traits? Why not just awaken directly to our essential soul and acquire it as our identity? If our goal is freedom, why not simply transcend our struggles?

It is true that someone who wrestles with a muddy person himself becomes muddy; when we wrestle with our negative traits, we expose ourselves to negativity and unsavory struggle. However, consider this scientific 'parable':

A study was conducted involving three mice. The first mouse was dropped into a bucket of water and allowed to flounder and nearly drowned before the researcher reached in and removed it from the water. The second mouse was dropped into an identical bucket, but was provided a small ladder; it floundered until it found the ladder and began to climb out. After much effort, this mouse saved itself from drowning. The third mouse was not immersed in water at all, but left in a peaceful, comfortable environment.

All three mice were measured repeatedly for biological signs of resilience and wellbeing. The first mouse, which had been saved by an outside force, had the lowest levels of resilience over time; its trauma persisted, and it became weak and sick. The second mouse, which had saved itself, had superior levels of resiliency, well-being, and strength — much greater even than the third mouse, which had not encountered the struggle and remained at peace. Because of its 'work', the existential challenge had strengthened the second mouse.

In a similar illustration, a man once watched a butterfly struggling for hours to exit its cocoon. In a moment of 'compassion', the man cut open the cocoon, allowing the butterfly to go free. This butterfly did not develop strong wings and was never able to fly. The labor of exiting the cocoon was difficult, but it had been the butterfly's true source of empowerment and freedom.

If we do not struggle to overcome compulsions and negative personality traits, we can't fully embody our essential soul. Relying on the safety and peace of complete transcendence actually weakens us and doesn't allow us to 'fly'. This does not mean that we should actively seek out difficulties and existential challenges. Mysteriously, our essential soul attracts to us exactly what we need in order to grow.

The Baal Shem Tov taught that we need to learn to "kiss" our challenges. We can lovingly and gratefully welcome challenges because when we overcome them, they create and reveal our essential character and our *Geulah Pratis* / individual redemption.

OUR EXPANDABLE CAPACITY

In terms of inner work and character development, we need to know that we are highly elastic and expandable, like a strong balloon. At any given point, it may look like we cannot contain any more challenges, but the truth is, the more inner work we take on, the more our capacity for growth expands. Our mind and inner narrative may tell us that our strength, willpower, time, or potential is limited, but we have much more ability than we think. Our 'mind' is merely our ego thinking that it is protecting us by keeping us 'comfortable' and complacent, but in truth, it is what is holding us back from our real potential.

If we put aside all limiting ideas and self-doubts, stop letting our mind dictate our potential, and simply take on more and more of life's challenges, we will find a capacity for truly heroic inner achievements. Of course, we should keep in mind that if we push ourselves too far, certainly if we do so too quickly, the 'balloon' may pop, and we can suffer emotional or even physical setbacks. One barometer that tells us if we are stretching ourselves too far is if we are no longer experiencing *Yishuv haDa'as* / settled mind and groundedness. It is actually rare for us to extend ourselves too far, more often, we are not extending ourselves enough.

In any case, as much as we push ourselves, we must remember that taking many small steps leads to covering long distances. As such, the more frequently we stretch ourselves the more elastic we become. Similarly, in terms of physical strength, the more we work our body, the more our body can accomplish. On an emotional level, the more we allow ourselves to be vulnerable and to express love, the more our capacity for love will expand. On an intellectual level, the more we push ourselves to learn, the more our mental capacity and neuroplasticity expands. Certainly, this dynamic is true as well on a spiritual level.

SMALL STEPS

Here is a 'mathematical' formula for success: Difficult ÷ Easy = Easy. That is, if you divide a large and difficult-looking task into small, easy steps, the entire task will become easy. For example, a person who desires to create a warm loving home and family, yet who still finds him or herself single, may feel that the project is so monumental as to be practically unattainable. However, the road to this destination is actually paved with many smaller, incremental steps forward. Such a person could begin with dating at least once a month, and affirming every day, "I am ready to meet my future spouse!" 'Laboring' in this way can lead to a sense of possibility, an inner victory, and eventually to an outward achievement as well.

Although a larger life goal might seem like an 'outer' issue, it is not. For, just as an 'external' situation may stimulate inner desperation, reactivity or a desire to give up, the reverse is also true—inner work can shift one's experience. Perceptions and feelings go together; the way we look at our situation is how it feels to us. Quieting the mind, dipping into transcendent presence, opening up to see the bigger picture, trusting in Reality, taking responsibility for our past, and hoping for the future, are all instrumental.

When one looks at their life with malaise, they may feel the drive to react by making drastic changes. They may begin to act boldly, but if they have set their sights too high, without concrete, attainable milestones, some parts of the journey will remain abstract and seemingly unattainable. In a short time, their boldness may wane, and they may collapse back into their old patterns of behavior.

Real change takes real work, and real work requires realistic goals. Realistic goals result from a functional understanding of our inner world. Grandiose resolutions are not the answer, rather, the key to sustainable growth is to patiently and consistently engage in 'small acts'. A small act can be an achievable goal that we set with regular reminders, such as saying to ourselves, 'Today, when I come home from work, I will give my child fifteen uninterrupted minutes of my time before doing anything else.' Or, 'Next time I go out with my friends or family, I will not look at my text messages.' Instead of impulsively declaring grandiose statements such as, 'I am going to be a better father or mother,' or 'I am going to be a more attentive friend,' declare a 'smaller' resolution such as, 'While I am with my child, I will refrain from looking at my phone for fifteen uninterrupted minutes.' Eventually, all of these 'small journeys' contribute to a bigger vision and greater goal.

SUCCESS BUILDS SUCCESS

In life, you win some, and you lose some, but with practice, you gradually lose less and less. Success breeds success. Start with small challenges that you know you can overcome, and build from there. When you feel successful in what you are doing, empowered and honest with yourself, you will have the strength and courage to continue.

In this 'process' paradigm of growth and development, you deal with your challenges head-on, and progress is often gradual and methodical. Addressing a challenge from the 'presence' paradigm, however, you don't contend with it head-on, rather you come from a place 'above' the challenge, and your success or growth manifests instantaneously.

STRUGGLING WITH THE PROBLEM OR BEING ABOVE PROBLEMS

When we are living exclusively in 'process' consciousness, we feel as if our problems and challenges are above us, and we need to fight to overcome them. If we have a lot of strength, we may be able to rise up and wage war against our problems head-on. This approach to life could be called the 'path of darkness', as the problems overshadow us, and we may even be 'in the dark' about their inner mechanics. We do not have enough awareness to see the whole picture as if from above. Thus, the compulsion, difficulty, or deficiency has the upper hand; we are to some extent 'controlled' by it, and we feel that we have an enormous amount of work to do. When we identify as our process-self, we feel fragmented and imperfect and are thus driven to relentlessly seek wholeness.

An opposite approach is 'the path of light', simply basking in the transcendent perfection and endless light of pure presence. The inner diamond-self is always whole to begin with, and will forever be.

Faced with a challenge such as temptation, we are faced with a dilemma; should we pursue the path of darkness and deal with the issue on the ground, on the level of the temptation itself? Or should we travel the path of light, immersed in the serenity of our 'inner perfection', rising above temptation altogether?

INNER WORK ON THE LEVEL OF PRESENCE: BEING

The 'path of darkness' is intent on pushing difficulties aside; it requires *Gevurah* / strength to overcome obstacles. In this mode of perception, we confront the *Kli* / 'vessel' or outer manifestation of the issue at hand, and strenuously attempt to push it away. The 'path of light' functions through *Chesed* / kindness. Although we do not fully or permanently 'retreat' into stillness and transcendent presence, awareness is key. Here we are not focusing on the future from a 'process' perspective, as in, 'I am broken and working to become whole in the future.' Rather, we stay rooted in our present awareness: 'I am *already* whole, and I am just dealing with an external brokenness. I am a pure soul, perfect just as I am. I am confident, I am capable, I am happy.' This is a redemptive state of consciousness, a consciousness of wholeness, light, and bliss.

The 'process' of meeting darkness head-on occurs within 'exile consciousness'; we see ourselves, too, as 'in the dark' or darkened — perhaps even broken or 'unholy' — and we are engaged in a battle to push that darkness away. This orientation is akin to the effortful 'work' that we might do on a weekday.

Entering the path of presence is like entering Shabbos (Shabbat), the day of light. To enter Shabbos, we need to be able to say (and feel), 'All my work is done. All is as it should be.' This is an expansive state of completeness in which we are at last able to see (and know) that we are essentially already redeemed.

Shabbos is a day of rest — of refraining from even thinking about 'work'. We do not attempt to push away shadows or struggle to change the future, we simply rest in a world of pure light, and present-moment positivity. As an effect, shadows and obstacles simply vanish. Then, when a new work week begins, if anything remains of those past difficulties, we can integrate and process them from a position of presence, positivity, refreshment, and strength.

Weekdays are generally an experience of *Olam HaZeh* / 'this world' of Yesh and process. Shabbos gives us a taste of *Olam HaBa* / 'the World to Come', the state of presence and redemption. In the path of 'Olam HaZeh', 'the path of darkness', we work on ourselves by arduously pushing aside temptations with all our *Gevurah* / strength. This inner work is also called *Avodah* / spiritual work "from below to above", putting in the effort to elevate our life higher and higher. In the path of 'Olam HaBa', 'the path of light', we simply let go into Divine Chesed, and allow the Infinite Light to dispel all darkness. This inner work, which is not really 'work' at all, requires no effort on our part. Our release from exile to redemption comes "from above to below," as it were.

WE ACT ACCORDING TO WHO WE THINK WE ARE

We tend to live up to what we imagine ourselves to be. People who argue in favor of their limitations — for example, 'I'm powerless because of my previous decisions, my low IQ, my difficult upbringing, my lack of education' — tend to remain in that limited definition. Even worse, defending your limitations will make you even more limited. Defining yourself only as your imperfect and evolving self will ensure that you will frequently fall in your struggles and struggle in your falls.

On the other hand, by nurturing our inner 'perfection', the image of our essential wholeness, we will find ourselves slipping and struggling less and less. In fact, we will become stronger and stronger, ethically, morally, and spiritually. Then, when we do slip, for example, when we become angry, our inner voice will automatically assert itself, 'It is not fitting for me, a wholesome and equanimous person, to act out in anger; I can solve this conflict from a higher perspective.' If we persistently envision ourselves as a pure soul of holy Light, of presence, wholeness, and incorruptible goodness expressed in a body, then reactivity will cease to be our default mode under pressure.

To realize and deepen our belief in our inner wholeness and goodness, it can help to repeat positive affirmations, such as, 'I am a good person,' 'I am an instrument of the Infinite Light.' Not only can this help our subconscious mind rewire itself and create an ingrained tendency to see ourselves as a whole person, but it can also help us act as the pure soul that we really are.

We may still slip up, but we will immediately see that our actions were out of character and do not define who we truly are. Eventually, our sense of wholeness will be imprinted in our deepest psyche, and our instinctive behavior will reflect this perfection.

UNIFYING PROCESS & PRESENCE

Human beings have an inborn desire to seek wholeness, reflecting the deeper wholeness that already exists within us. Similarly, our ability to rise and return from transcendence is an indication of the dynamic nature of our essence. The deepest part of us holds and integrates both 'process' and 'presence', finite and infinite, *Yesh* / some-thing-ness and *Ayin* / nothing-ness, darkness and Light. In this way, the dilemma of whether to work to overcome a challenge or simply to rise above it is a false dilemma. We should approach every challenge, temptation, or difficulty from a third standpoint: that of our essence-self. By embodying 'essence' we can both confront and remain above our challenges. We can engage in the work of 'process' while remaining rooted in the world of 'presence' and perfection.

INNER WORK ON THE LEVEL OF UNIFIED PROCESS & PRESENCE

On the path of essence, we are paradoxically 'becoming' *and* 'being', imperfect *and* perfect, body *and* soul, finite *and* infinite. We do not dismiss, rationalize, or overlook our pain or negative tendencies, the chaotic side of the world around us, nor the needs of others. As essence, we both transcend and include the dialectic of darkness and light together.

On the one hand, we recognize we are perfect, the 'work' has already been done, and there is 'nothing to do'. This is not a path of sifting out sparks of light and discarding darkness. Rather, it is a path of *Yichud* / unity, connecting with everything, both the light and the darkness, in all of life's multitudinous unity.

Here, we do not hide from or deny our pain, and we do not dismiss the darkness and demons; rather, we acknowledge them as real in our Yesh reality. We do not run from feelings of pain and suffering, as from the standpoint of essence, these, too, are part of our soul's experience, and thus, we are not afraid of them. We stand within and above them and can and will master them. We are cognizant that we are not defined by our limitations or addictions, yet we have compassion for our lower self as it struggles with its negative habits and hurts.

From a standpoint above our struggles, we are able to create a *Yichud* / unification with them in a way that stimulates our growth and reveals the light implicit within darkness. In other words, when we identify as the witnessing self, equanimously observing all the drama unfolding on the level of process, we remain existentially higher than all temptations and triggers that may rise into consciousness, and from there, we can perform or acknowledge a *Yichud* / unity with them without being dragged down by them.

In practical terms, being in essence-consciousness allows us to successfully engage the practice and inner work of *Iskafyah* / 'refraining' from triggers, from a place of radical presence. This inner work is done for the purpose of *Is'hapchah* / transformation, and harnessing the power of those triggers for the good — and ultimately, there is only good. In this path, we eventually reach a point where we can see all of our experiences and dramas of life as a *Berachah* / blessing, revealing previously concealed *Kedushah* / holiness and nobility.

Paradoxical as it may sound, on the level of essence, our efforts in the practice of Iskafya come from a place of enduring wholeness, light, and presence. In the world of the process-self, we attempt to break a strong *Ta'avah* / desire in order to *become* bigger. On the path of darkness, when we identify as a person who is addicted to or overwhelmed by pain, a person who is struggling with darkness and demons, by refraining from and pushing aside our reactivity, we *become* a bigger, holier, less addictive, nobler person. However, as we enter the path of essence and unity, we break our dependencies and heal our pain not in order to *become* bigger but rather to reveal to ourselves that we have *always* been bigger.

For example, every morning, you wake up, and soon thereafter you 'must' have your perfect coffee, for without it, so you tell yourself, your day will feel a little off-kilter, and you'll be irritated and impatient with your co-workers. Your self-talk, your inner narrative in this scenario, is giving into a smallness, as proven by the following situation.

One day, you wake up, and your coffee machine is broken. It just happens to be a very important day in your career, so you gather yourself up, and instead of telling yourself you'll be irritable, you tell yourself, 'I did not have my perfect coffee today, but I can still be the bigger person!' You go to work *as if* you have had your special coffee, and amazingly, you manage to stay focused, calm, and forgiving for the entire day. On one level, you have broken an 'addictive pattern' and made yourself a little bigger than the day before. On a deeper level, you have shown yourself that you are *essentially* bigger than this, that your equilibrium and state of mind is *never* dependent on the coffee or any mood-altering substances or conditions. You, *yourself,* are bigger than you could ever imagine.

Here, in the path of essence, we have the strength to honestly acknowledge our smallness and struggles because we are bigger than them. We are present with our process. The Yesh of suffering is not separate from the bliss of Ayin; the stillness of being is not canceled out by the movement of becoming. We are always already redeemed — even amid exile.

With the dawning of this realization, Divine healing flows through us and then on to others, as clear, wise, and truly life-affirming choices become available, perhaps for the first time.

06

AFTERWORD:

LIVING AWAKE AND
SEEING ALIVENESS EVERYWHERE

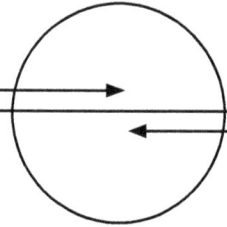

I T IS AN UNFORTUNATE TRUTH OF OUR CURRENT MOMENT THAT
many people live with a gnawing sense of deep fear and panic.
They live as if surrounded by a wild, untamed jungle, projectiles
being thrown at them continuously and from every direction, and
their only choices are to fight or flee, or to 'freeze' in dissociative
behaviors. Such a life is lived as if in a gun duel — on is either
"killed," or "killing." Whoever is quicker on the draw wins.

Even many self-styled spiritual mentors and life coaches
feel an anxious need to outrace their competition through exaggerated advertising, carefully airbrushed public images, and

hypnotic sales techniques, all to ensure that they can aggressively inflate their prices. People begin to look a bit like birds pecking at seeds; between every peck at the earth, they raise their heads in hypervigilance to make sure no one will threaten them or steal their little cache of food.

While not ideal, such an existence is at least alive, awake, or 'happy' on some level; and not merely mechanical. There is, however, an even more restricted state of being, and those who live in an even more contracted state of functioning and consciousness. These people unfortunately live their lives robotically and reactively.

Remember the old pinball game in arcades? It's a great metaphor for this way of life. The things that happen to us are the ball, which keeps bouncing down towards us and nearly plummeting into the 'out hole' or trough. In this context, the object of the game of life is to constantly and reactively swipe the flippers to bat the ball upwards, gaining another moment of relative calm until it all comes tumbling back at us again.

In this cruel game, there is never time to think, contemplate, plan, pray, or rest. The moment you let your hands off the flipper buttons, the ball may shoot down the drain, and it is 'Game over'. Yet, whenever you hit the ball from one side, it sets off a series of rapid ricochets, and it comes back at a different angle. One day you don't feel well, and you hit the ball upwards and manage to survive that day, but the next day another problem comes falling toward you from another direction, and now your child is having issues at school. Perhaps you are overcharged on your account, your insurance policy won't cover something, there's a flood, a worrisome war, or a local tragedy, every day another drama blows up in front of you, and often hitting the ball in one direction causes a chain of unexpected consequences. At some point, you realize you are perpetually responding to crises and issues full-time.

In this mode, every time you react and hit the ball, there's a counter-reaction coming back at you, often with even greater force and from an unexpected direction. One day your boss speaks to you with frustration, and you can't keep your anger under wraps, so you react with vengeance and resign on the spot. Of course, you are for a moment relieved by reactively hitting this falling ball upwards, yet the ball soon comes pounding down even harder, for now you are out of a job. Your rent becomes too expensive, so you react again and move to a cheaper place to live, but now you are lonely without nearby friends. You impulsively swipe at the ball again and again, mechanically and robotically, as it seems like there is nothing else to do.

LEVELS OF RESPONSE

There are four grades of existence: the mineral, vegetable, animal, and human worlds. Parallel to these there are four ways we can respond to what life deals us, corresponding to four states of consciousness. The lowest response is mechanical or inanimate ('mineral'), and the highest response is fully conscious, awake, and alive ('human'). Who we are affects the way we observe the world and how it appears and responds to us. Hence, the more awake and alive we are, the more the world around us will be alive and hopeful and giving in our experience. Conversely, the more 'inanimate' we are, the more closed off and stuck, and the more the world around us will seem dead, dark, hopeless, and ungiving.

This becomes a loop: the more the world appears hopeful and kind, the more proactive and kind our responses to the world become. The more the world appears hopeless and unkind, the more reactive and unkind the energy and behavior that flows from us is. If we feel that we are a mere cog in a mechanical universe, we will respond to life mechanically, and our life will feel random, without purpose.

The more we react blindly or even unintentionally to events, the more life will seem to come at us blindly and unintentionally.

THE MORE WE LIVE WITH INTENTION THE MORE INTENTIONAL THE WORLD APPEARS

If we wish to see the world as more alive and pregnant with possibility, it behooves us to become more alive and awake. To observe the meaningfulness and intentionality of everything that happens to us, we need to increase our *Da'as* / conscious awareness. We need to let go of the handles of the pinball game, as it were, and deeply observe ourselves and discern who we really are.

Higher than the 'mineral-self' is the vegetative self, which is more supple and open to growth and self-propagation. Here, life is not merely a mechanical pinball game; one does not act rashly in ever-increasing frustration. Here one is able to open themselves to receive the sunlight, water, and nutrients of the soil. Higher yet is 'animal' consciousness, with a will to strategize and work for survival, to store food for the winter, and to nurture our young.

It is only when we are fully aware as a human being, with mindful, non-reactive intentionality, that the world around us also seems filled with mindfulness and intention. The world of clear *Hashgacha* / Divine providence becomes revealed to us. The more we live with our own *Hashgacha* / intentionality and focus, the more Hashgacha in the world is shown to us. Everything begins to feel alive, purposeful, and catered exactly to what we need at any given moment. When you live this way, the wider world parallels your own inner world and you begin to see how everything that is happening in your life is exactly how it should be. Nothing is random or 'thrown at you'.

Of course, you may still be filled with earnest questions, such as, 'Is this the only way I could have learned this lesson?' But overall, your story begins to make sense, and the feeling of randomness falls away. Life no longer seems to be coming at you, a victim that needs to react, rather, life seems to be happening 'for' you, and you have the presence of mind to respond thoughtfully and consciously. You are not a victim of life, but rather, a co-creator. You live your particular life with Hashgacha, and the world responds and offers you a world of Cosmic Hashgacha.

When we live intentionally, we are tapping into the purity of presence in all processes. From the space of stillness, we engage with a world of movement, progress, possibility, and hope. When we let go, take a deep breath, and mindfully choose actions that will bring beneficial outcomes, we are able to solve challenges with strength, aliveness, confidence, and joy. The world then echoes our essential happiness back to us. As we come alive, all phenomena come alive for us, offering us an array of possible futures, and we naturally lean into the wonderful future that is coming.

The way of Light and Essence first dawns within ourselves, and then within everyone around us.

Only together will we become true human beings: alive, present, alert, engaged, mindful, and caring, just as we were created to be. The entire world will then enter a more redemptive state, sparkling with hope and love, burgeoning with acts of goodness and authenticity, an ever-unfolding tapestry of friendship, nourishment, and peace in all the worlds. ☙

Other Books by Rav Pinson

Rav Pinson on the Torah

AWAKENINGS:
Drawing Life from the Weekly Torah Reading

The deeper teachings of the Torah reveal to us that the weekly Torah reading is connected to the unique energetic properties of that week. Every Torah portion, and thus every week, radiates with a particular quality, a distinct energy that, when understood and received, can bring tremendous guidance and assistance to every facet of our lives.

Delving into the weekly Torah reading and uncovering its overarching theme allows us to apply the power available on that week in our practical life.

We can learn how to harness the Ko'ach, power, of each unique Torah reading to expand consciousness, overcome challenges, gain control of our lives, and come to learn how to serve Hashem, self and others more mindfully, productively and effectively.

Weaving together the various facets of Torah interpretation, from the most esoteric (Kabbalah) and mystical (Chassidus) to the straightforward literal meaning (Peshat), this book is a multi-dimensional tapestry of practical, allegorical, philosophical, and mystical ideas and implications.

Rav Pinson on the Life Cycle

A BOND FOR ETERNITY
Understanding the Bris Milah

What is the Bris Milah – the covenant of circumcision? What does it represent, symbolize and signify? This book provides an in depth and sensitive review of this fundamental Mitzvah. In this little masterpiece of wisdom – profound yet accessible —the deeper meaning of this essential rite of passage and its eternal link to the Jewish people, is revealed and explored.

UPSHERNISH: THE FIRST HAIRCUT
Exploring the Laws, Customs & Meanings
of a Boy's First Haircut

What is the meaning of Upsherin, the traditional celebration of a boy's first haircut at the age of three? Why is a boy's hair allowed to grow freely for his first three years? What is the deeper import of hair in all its lengths and varieties? What is the meaning of hair coverings? Includes a guide to conducting an Upsherin ceremony.

THE JEWISH WEDDING:
A Guide to the Rituals and Traditions
of the Wedding Ceremony

The Jewish Wedding: A Guide to the Rituals and Traditions of the Wedding Ceremony.

This guide is based on the teachings of Torah, Talmud, Medrash, Zohar, Halacha, Poskim, Kabbalah and Chassidus. By quoting these teachings, we actively draw down the 'presence' of these holy souls who revealed these teachings, thus extending blessings to the bride and groom and all in attendance at the Chupa.

THE MYSTERY OF KADDISH
Understanding the Mourner's Kaddish

The Mystery of Kaddish is an in-depth exploration into the Mourner's Prayer. Throughout Jewish history, there have been many rites and rituals associated with loss and mourning, yet none have prevailed quite like the Mourner's Kaddish Prayer, which has become the definitive ritual of mourning. The book explores the source of this prayer and deconstructs the meaning to better understand the grieving process and how the Kaddish prayer supports and uplifts the bereaved through their own personal journey to healing.

———————

THE BOOK OF LIFE AFTER LIFE

What is a soul? What happens to us after we physically die?

What is consciousness, and can it survive without a physical brain?

Can we remember our past lives?

Do near-death experiences prove immortality?

What is Gan Eden? Resurrection?

Exploring the possibility of surviving death, the near-death experience and a glimpse into what awaits us after this life.

(This book is an updated and expanded version of the book; Jewish Wisdom of the Afterlife)

Rav Pinson on Kabbalah

REINCARNATION AND JUDAISM
The Journey of the Soul

A fascinating analysis of the concept of Gilgul / Reincarnation. Dipping into the fountain of ancient wisdom and modern understanding, this book addresses and answers such basic questions as: What is reincarnation? Why does it occur? And how does it affect us personally?

INNER RHYTHMS
The Kabbalah of Music

Exploring the inner dimension of sound and music, and particularly, how music permeates all aspects of life. The topics range from Deveikus/Unity and Yichudim/Unifications, to the more personal issues, such as Simcha/Happiness and Marirus/ sadness.

THIRTY–TWO GATES OF WISDOM
Into the Heart of Kabbalah & Chassidus

What is Kabbalah? And what are the differences between the theoretical, meditative, magical and personal Kabbalistic teachings? What are the four paths of interpreting the teachings of the ARIzal? What did Chassidus teach? These are some of the fundamental issues expanded upon in this text. And then, more specifically, why are there so many names of G-d and what do they represent? What are the key concepts of these deeper teachings?

The book explores the grand narrative of the great chain of reality, how there was and is a movement from the Infinite Oneness of Hashem to a world of (apparent) duality and multiplicity.

————

PASSPORT TO KABBALAH
A Journey of Inner Transformation

Life is a journey full of ups and downs, inside-outs, and unexpected detours. There are times when we think we know exactly where we want to be headed, and other times when we are so lost we don't even know where we are. This slim book provides readers with a passport of sorts to help them through any obstacles along their path of self-refinement, reflection, and self-transformation.

————

SEVEN PATHS TO LOVE, LIFE, PURPOSE & SERENITY:
A Book on the Sheva Mitzvos

————

THE GARDEN OF PARADOX:
The Essence of Non - Dual Kabbalah

This book is a Primer on the Essential Philosophy of Kabbalah presented as a series of 3 conversations, revealing the mysteries of Creator, Creation and Consciousness. With three representational students, embodying respectively, the philosopher, the activist and the mystic, the book, tackles the larger questions of life. Who is G-d? Who am I? Why do I exist? What is my purpose in this life? Written in clear and concise prose, the text, gently guides the reader towards making sense of life's paradoxes and living meaningfully.

————

THE POWER OF CHOICE:
A Practical Guide to Conscious Living

It is the essential premise of this book that we hold the key to unlock many of the gates that seem closed to us and keep us from living our fullest life. That key we all hold is the power to choose. The Power of Choice is the primary tool that we have at our disposal to impact the world and effect change within our own lives. We often give up this power to outside forces such as the market, media, politicians or peer pressure; or to internal forces that often function beyond our conscious control such as ego, anger, lust, greed or jealousy. Making conscious, compassionate and creative decisions is the cornerstone of living a mature and meaningful life.

MYSTIC TALES FROM THE EMEK HAMELECH

Mystic Tales of the Emek HaMelech, is a wondrous and inspiring collection of stories culled from the Emek HaMelech. Emek HaMelech, from which these stories have been taken, (as well as its author) is a bit of a mystery. But like all good mysteries, it is one worth investigating. In this spirit the present volume is being offered to the general public in the merit and memory of its saintly author, as well as in the hopes of introducing a vital voice of deeper Torah teaching and tradition to a contemporary English speaking audience

---

Rav Pinson on Meditation

MEDITATION AND JUDAISM
Exploring the Jewish Meditative Paths

A comprehensive work encompassing the entire spectrum of Jewish thought, from the sages of the Talmud and the early Kabbalists to the modern philosophers and Chassidic masters. This book is both a scholarly, in-depth study of meditative practices, and a practical, easy to follow guide for any person interested in meditating the Jewish way.

TOWARD THE INFINITE

A book focusing exclusively on the Chassidic approach to meditation known as Hisbonenus. Encompassing the entire meditative experience, it takes the reader on a comprehensive and engaging journey through this unique practice. The book explores the various states of consciousness that a person encounters in the course of the meditation, beginning at a level of extreme self-awareness and concluding with a state of total non-awareness.

BREATHING & QUIETING THE MIND

Achieving a sense of self-mastery and inner freedom demands that we gain a measure of hegemony over our thoughts. We learn to choose out thoughts so that we are not at the mercy of whatever belches up to the mind. Through quieting the mind and conscious breathing we can slow the onrush of anxious, scattered thinking and come to a deeper awareness of the interconnectedness of all of life.

Source texts are included in translation, with how-to-guides for the various practices.

SOUND AND VIBRATION:
Tuning into the Echoes of Creation

Through our perception of sound and vibration we internalize the world around us. What we hear, and how we process that hearing, has a profound impact on how we experience life. What we hear can empower us or harm us. A defining human capacity is to harness the power sound -- through speech, dialogue, and song, and through listening to others. Hearing is primary dimension of our existence. In fact, as a fetus our ears were the first fully operating sensory organs to develop.

This book will guide you in methods of utilizing the power of sound and vibration to heal and maintain mental, emotional and spiritual health, to fine-tune your Midos and even to guide you into deeper levels of Deveikus / conscious unity with Hashem. The vibratory patterns of the Aleph-Beis are particularly useful portals into our deeper conscious selves. Through chanting and deep listening, we can use the letters and sounds to shift our very mindset, to induce us into a state of presence and spiritual elevation.

VISUALIZATION AND IMAGERY:
Harnessing the Power of our Mind's Eye

We assume that what we see with our eyes is absolute. Yet, beyond our ability to choose what we see, we have the ability to choose how we see. This directly translates into how we experience life. In a world saturated with visual imagery, our senses are continuously assaulted with Kelipa/empty/fantasy imagery that we would not necessarily choose. These images can negatively affect our relationship with ourselves, with the world around us, and with the Divine. This volume seeks to show us how we can alter that which we observe through harnessing the power of our mind's eye, the inner sanctum of our imagination. We thus create a new way to see and experience the world. This book teaches us how to utilize visualization and imagery as a way to develop our spiritual sensitivity and higher intuition, and ultimately achieve Deveikus/Unity with Hashem.

Rav Pinson on The Holidays

THE HAGGADAH:
Pathways to Pesach and the Haggadah

"In every generation a person must regard oneself as having gone out of Mitzrayim / Egypt." This means that when recalling the Exodus, which occurred thousands of years ago, we also need to envision ourselves as being taken out of Mitzrayim and freed from enslavement.

Introducing the Haggadah and the themes of Pesach, this book delves into the greater context of the Festival and the Seder, allowing us to tap into the profound inspiration and Koach / power that Pesach and Seder Night offers.

EIGHT LIGHTS
8 Meditations for Chanukah

What is the meaning and message of Chanukah? What is the spiritual significance of the Lights of the Menorah? What are the Lights telling us? What is the deeper dimension of the Dreidel? Rav Pinson, with his trademark deep learning and spiritual sensitivity guides us through eight meditations relating to the Lights of the Menorah, the eight days of Chanukah, and a fascinating exploration of the symbolism and structure of the Dreidel. Includes a detailed how-to guide for lighting the Chanukah Menorah.

THE PURIM READER
The Holiday of Purim Explored

With a Persian name, a masquerade dress code and a woman as the heroine, Purim is certainly unusual amongst the Jewish holidays. Most people are very familiar with the costumes, Megilah and revelry, but are mystified by their significance. This book offers a glimpse into the hidden world of Purim, uncovering these mysteries and offering a deeper understanding of this unique holiday.

The High Holiday Series:

A CALL TO MAJESTY:
The Mysteries of Shofar & Rosh Hashanah

The Shofar is the preeminent symbol of Rosh Hashanah, waking us up to a time of deep introspection and celebration. But why do we blow the Shofar on this most special of days? While the Torah decrees that the Shofar must be blown, it does not provide a reason. On the deepest level, the Shofar is of course beyond reason altogether, and yet, from within its shape, sound and story, a constellation of "reasons" emerge. Rebirth. Responsibility. Radical Amazement. On a primal vibrational level, the Shofar calls each of us to a place of deeper consciousness and community as we crown the King of All Creation.

A CALL TO MAJESTY delves deeply into the world of Rosh Hashanah and its primary Mitzvah, the sound of the Shofar. Weaving together a multi-dimensional tapestry of practical, allegorical, philosophical, and mystical ideas and implications, the teachings collected herein empower us all to answer the higher calling of the Shofar.

A LIGHTNESS OF BEING:
Your Guide to Yom Kippur

Yom Kippur is unabashedly transformative; the power of the day beckons us to work toward fundamental transformation and Teshuvah / return to who we really are. Often, the word Teshuvah is unfortunately translated as 'repentance'. It is more accurately rendered as 'return', meaning both a return 'from' our states of spiritual alienation and exile, as well as a 'turning to' experiencing our deepest selves. Yom Kippur empowers us to return to our essence, reclaim who we truly are, and live from that place.

A LIGHTNESS OF BEING delves into the powerful and transformative day of Yom Kippur. Weaving together a multi-dimensional tapestry of practical, allegorical, philosophical and mystical ideas and implications, the teachings gathered herein empower us all to enter Yom Kippur and truly feel enlightened, elevated, lighter and transformed.

———————

THE FOUR SPECIES
The Symbolism of the Lulav & Esrog

The Four Species have inspired countless commentaries and traditions and intrigued scholars and mystics alike. In this little masterpiece of wisdom both profound and practical - the deep symbolic roots and nature of the Four Species are explored. The Na'anuim, or ritual of the Lulav movement, is meticulously detailed and Kavanos,, are offered for use with the practice. Includes an illustrated guide to the Lulav Movements.

Rav Pinson on Prayer

———————

INNER WORLDS OF JEWISH PRAYER

A Guide to Develop and Deepen
the Prayer Experience

While much attention has been paid to the poetry, history, theology and contextual meaning of the prayers, the intention of this work is to provide a guide to finding meaning and effecting transformation through the prayer experience itself.

Explore: *What happens when we pray? *How do we enter the mind-state of prayer? *Learning to incorporate the body into the prayers. *Discover techniques to enhance and deepen prayer and make it a transformative experience.

This empowering and inspiring text, demonstrates how through proper mindset, preparation and dedication, the experience of prayer can be deeply transformative and ultimately, life-altering.

———————

ILLUMINATED SOUND:
The Baal Shem Tov on Prayer

In the year 1698 a great light was revealed to the world with the descent of the holy soul of the Baal Shem Tov. In time, the Baal Shem Tov became one of the most important and influential teachers of Torah in all of history, and the founder of Chassidus.

Amongst the vast repository of profound and revolutionary teachings of the holy Baal Shem Tov, the teachings on the path of Tefilah / Prayer are the most elaborate. The teachings of the Baal Shem Tov on Tefilah include some of his most innovative expressions, or Chidushim. Tefilah is the essential and central tenet from which all other teachings flow.

In this masterful and practical text, Rav Pinson revives the awe-inspiring and transformational teachings of the Baal Shem Tov, and illuminates his unique path to Tefilah.

Rav Pinson on Jewish Practice

RECLAIMING THE SELF
The Way of Teshuvah

Teshuvah is one of the great gifts of life. It speaks of a hope for a better today and empowers us to choose a brighter tomorrow. But what exactly is Teshuvah? How does it work? How can we undo our past and how do we deal with guilt? And what is healthy regret without eroding our self-esteem? In this fascinating and empowering book, the path for genuine transformation and a way to include all of our past in the powerful moment of the now, is explored and demonstrated.

WRAPPED IN MAJESTY
Tefillin - Exploring the Mystery

Tefillin, the black boxes and leather straps that are worn during prayer, are curiously powerful and mysterious. Within the inky black boxes lie untold secrets. In this profound, passionate and thought-provoking text, the multi-dimensional perspectives of Tefillin are explored and revealed. Magically weaving together all levels of Torah including the Peshat (literal observation), to Remez (allegorical), to Derush, (homiletic), to Sod (hidden) into one beautiful tapestry. Inspirational and instructive, Wrapped in Majesty: Tefillin, will make putting on the Tefillin more meaningful and inspiring.

SECRETS OF THE MIKVAH:
Waters of Transformation

A Mikvah is a pool of water used for the purpose of ritual immersion; a place where one moves from a state of Tumah; impurity, blockage and death—to a place of Teharah; purity, fluidity and life.

In SECRETS OF THE MIKVAH, Rav Pinson delves into the transformative powers of the Mikvah with his trademark all-encompassing perspective that ranges from the literal, Pshat observation and Halachic implications of the texts, to the allegorical, the philosophical, and finally, to the deep secrets of the Mikvah as revealed by Kabbalah and Chassidus.

This insightful and inspirational text demonstrates how immersion in a Mikvah can be a transformative and life-altering practice, and includes various Kavanos—deep intentions—for all people, through various stages of life, that empower and enrich the immersion experience.

THE MYSTERY OF SHABBOS
Shabbat Rediscovered

Delving into the transformative power of Shabbos. With an all-encompassing perspective that ranges from the literal, Pshat observation and Halachic implications of the texts, to the allegorical, the philosophical, and finally, to the deeper secrets as revealed by Kabbalah and Chassidus, creating an elegant tapestry of thought and experience. THE MYSTERY OF SHABBOS is a profound meditation on the meaning of Shabbos and demonstrates the physical, emotional, mental and spiritual possibilities available and given to us with the gift of Shabbos. Studying and contemplating this inspired text on the depths of Shabbos will unveil a redemptive light in your experience of the Seventh Day -- and by extension, every day of your life.

Rav Pinson on Time

THE SPIRAL OF TIME:
A 12 Part Series on the Months of the Year

VOL 1: THE SPIRAL OF TIME:
Unraveling the Yearly Cycle

Many centuries ago, the Sages of Israel were the foremost authority in the fields of both astronomical calculation and astrological wisdom, including the deeper interpretations of the cycles and seasons. Over time, this wisdom became hidden within the esoteric teachings of the Torah, and as a result was known only to students and scholars of the deepest depths of the tradition. More recently, the great teachers, from R.Yitzchak Luria (the Arizal) to the Baal Shem Tov, taught that as the world approaches the Era of Redemption, it is a Mitzvah / spiritual obligation to broadly reveal this wisdom.

"The Spiral of Time" is volume 1 is a series of 12 books, and serves as an introductory book to the basic concepts and nature of the Hebrew calendar and explores the special day of Rosh Chodesh.

VOL 2: THE MONTH OF NISAN:
Miraculous Awakenings from Above

The month of NISAN is the first month of the lunar cycle of the year, a month that brings in the spring and a month of redemption. Spring represents a time of plenty, abundance, sunshine, hope, and possibility. Redemption, on whatever level, feels palpable and accessible. In spring, the world is redeemed from the cold winter, the flower is redeemed from the tree, the grass from the earth, and we too feel that redemption is possible. A whole complex of ideas, including newness, redemption, going out of Egypt, and being freed from slavery, is intricately bound with the idea of Aviv / spring and the powerful month of Nisan.

VOL 3: THE MONTH OF IYYAR:
EVOLVING THE SELF
& The Holiday of LAG B'OMER

The month of IYYAR is the second month of the spring, a month that connects the Redemption from Egypt in Nissan with the Revelation of Torah in Sivan. The Chai/ Eighteenth day of the Month is the day we celebrate the Rashbi (Rabbi Shimon Bar Yochai) and the revealing of the hidden aspects of the Torah. This is the 'Holiday' of Lag b'Omer. The book explores the unique quality of this special month, a month that has a Mitzvah of counting the Omer every day. In addition, the book explores the roots and significance of the mystical 'holiday' of Lag b'Omer. Including the customs & Practices of Lag b'Omer, such as, bonfires, bows & arrows, parades, Upsherin, and more.

VOL 4: THE MONTH OF SIVAN:
The Art of Receiving: Shavuos and Matan Torah

Sivan is the third month of the lunar cycle. One is a singularity. Two is division. Three is harmony, a unity that synthesizes individuality and multiplicity, Heaven and Earth, Spirituality and Physicality. During this month we celebrate Shavuos and the giving of the Torah, the ultimate expression of the unity of the Above and Below and we aspire to connect with the Keser/Crown of Torah that Transcends and yet includes all Worlds. Learning how to truly receive Higher wisdom in our Lower faculties is the mental, emotional, and spiritual exercise of the month.

VOL 5: THE MONTHS OF TAMUZ AND AV:
Embracing Brokenness -
17th of Tamuz, Tisha B'Av, & Tu B'Av

Each month and season of the year, radiates with distinct Divine qualities and unique opportunities for growth and Tikkun.

The summer month of Tamuz and Av contain the longest and hottest days of the year. The raised temperature is indicative of a corresponding spiritual heat, a time of harsher judgement and potential destruction, such as the destructions of the first and second Beis HaMikdash, which began on the 17th of Tamuz and culminated on the 9th and 10th of Av.

A few days later, on Tu b'Av, the darkness is transformed and reveals the greatest light and possibility for new life. During these summer months of Tamuz and Av we embrace our brokenness so that we can heal and transform darkness into light.

VOL 6: THE MONTH OF ELUL:
Days of Introspection and Transformation

Each month of the year radiates with a distinct quality and provides unique opportunities for growth and personal transformation. Elul, as the final month of the spring/summer season is connected to endings. Elul gives us the strength to be able to finish strong, to end well. Elul also serves as a month of preparation for the New Year/Rosh Hashanah.

We inhale our past year, ending with wisdom and then we also gain the wisdom to begin anew and exhale a positive year into being. The mental, emotional, and spiritual objective of this month is introspection and the reclaiming of our inner purity and wholeness.

VOL 7: THE MONTH OF TISHREI:
A Time of Rebirth & Upward Movement

Each month of the year radiates with distinct Divine qualities and unique opportunities for growth and spiritual illumination. As Tishrei begins the new yearly cycle, it is an appropriate month to introspect, reflect and resolve to move forward and preserve moving forward into the more inward months of the winter. This month creates the space to unburden ourselves from our negativities, and enter a more sacred, grounded sacred space. In Tishrei we are given the gift of forgiveness and then the ability to truly regain our space and inner joy.

VOL 8: THE MONTH OF CHESHVAN:
Navigating Transitions, Elevating the Fall

Directly on the heels of the inspiring and holiday-filled month of Tishrei, Cheshvan is a month that is quiet and devoid of holidays. In the month of Cheshvan we use the stored up energies of the previous months to self-generate our inspiration and creativity and provide ourselves with the strength to rise up after a fall. In Cheshvan we are entering into a stormier, wetter and colder season. It is a month of transition. The mental, emotional and spiritual objective of this month is to weather the transitions, learn to self-generate and stand tall. And if we do fall, we use the quality of this month to get back up and do so with more conviction, strength, wisdom and clarity.

VOL 9: THE MONTH OF KISLEV:
Rekindling Hope, Dreams and Trust

Kislev is the final month of the fall. Throughout this month, daylight progressively shortens, and the temperatures drop. Towards the end of the month, at the darkest hour, the winter solstice arrives and we begin the celebration of Chanukah. We commemorate the miracle of a small jug of oil that burned for eight nights, and as we celebrate, daylight expands. In the month of Kislev-despite the darkness, or perhaps because of it-we have the ability to tap into the Ohr HaGanuz, the hidden light of hope that rekindles our dreams and aspirations.

VOL 10: THE MONTH OF TEVES:
Refining Relationships, Elevating the Body

The quality of Teves is generally harsh—much like its counterpart Tamuz in the summer, thus the tendency for many is to hunker down, retract, curl up and wait for the month to pass by, only to reemerge when the harshness has dissipated. Think for a moment about the 'easier' months of the year, which, like gentle waves in the ocean, carry us where we want to go. We can ride these energies easily and they can propel us forward effortlessly, we just need to go with the overall flow, so to speak. The harsher months, on the other hand, can be compared to the more powerful waves that emanate from the belly of the ocean,which come forcefully crashing down and can easily drown a person before they even realize what has happened. However, those who want to utilize the momentum of the powerful energy that is available during such times can, with caution and creativity, harness these intense waves and ride them higher and farther than other, more gentle circumstances may allow. However, harnessing the power of Tohu, the raw energy of the body, does in fact need to be approached with great care and attention.

VOL 11: THE MONTH OF SHEVAT: ELEVATING EATING
& The Holiday of Tu b'Shevat

Each month of the year radiates with a distinct Divine energy and thus unique opportunities for growth, *Tikkun* and illumination. According to the deeper teachings of the Torah, all of these distinct qualities, opportunities and natural phenomena correspond to a certain data set. That is, the nature of each month is elucidated by a specific letter of the Aleph Beis, a tribe, verse, human sense, and so forth. The month of Shevat is particularly connected to food and our relationship to bodily intake. During this month we celebrate Tu b'Shevat, the New Year of the Tree, and aspire to create a proper and physically/emotionally/spiritually healthy relationship with food.

VOL 12: THE MONTH OF ADAR:
Transformation Through Laughter & Holy Doubt

Each month of the year radiates with distinct Divine qualities and unique opportunities for growth and spiritual illumination. As Adar concludes the monthly cycle of the year, as well as the solar phenomena of the winter, it is an appropriate month to think about our essential identity, before moving out to meet the world come spring. This month we strive to create a healthy relationship with holy humor, unbounded joy, and a general sense of lightness of being. Through the work of Adar we transform negative, crippling doubt and uncertainties into radical wonderment and openness.

www.ingramcontent.com/pod-product-compliance
Lightning Source LLC
Chambersburg PA
CBHW040421110426
42813CB00014B/2725